Beyond Educational Injustices

*The Long Journey after Emancipation to Achieve
Secondary and Post-Secondary Education*

Beyond Educational Injustices

*The Long Journey after Emancipation
to Achieve Secondary and Post-Secondary Education*

Joan-Yvette Campbell

"Slavery is one of the worst forms of violence – as is the denial of education. Education is key to liberating children from slavery."

– **Kailash Satyarthi**

Table of Contents

Dedication

Beyond Educational Injustices is dedicated to my father, Renford E. Campbell. He was born in 1931 in Portland, Jamaica. He and his educational experiences were an inspiration in writing the book. My father was one of those children who grew up during the colonial era when secondary education was not an option for poor children of African descent like himself. The closest secondary school located in his parish was founded during the slavery era, so its main purpose was to provide education to those whites who could not afford a private education or to go overseas to study. For many years after the abolition of slavery, the school continued to cater to the ruling white minority and biracial children whose parents could afford to pay their tuition. My father's inability to attend high school in his parish did not prevent him from persisting with his dreams to continue his education. Therefore, he moved to the capital city of Kingston so he could enroll in the public technical high school. However due to financial reasons, he later dropped out and returned to his native parish. His early departure from high school did not prevent his yearning to continue learning throughout his life by taking whatever opportunities he could to grasp knowledge on his own or though on-the-job training, seminars, and workshops. He grew into a man with a wealth of knowledge that allowed him to engage in hearty conversations on a variety of local and worldwide topics with family, friends, and those strangers he met along the way. So, the restrictions that hampered him from gaining a secondary education during the colonial era did not curtail his continued life-long desire to learn. My father passed away peacefully on January 30th, 2018. We miss the knowledge he imparted on so many that surpassed the

British colonial rulers' low learning expectations for people of African descent during his generation. My father's educational experiences represent the multitude of people not only in Jamaica but others of African descent in the Caribbean, South and Central America, and the United States who experienced a system where they were denied the right to continue their education past the elementary level. He is symbolic of many who lived under colonial educational restrictions yet still achieved a high standard of learning. As you read ***Beyond Educational Injustices***, consider not only my father's experiences but also be a torchbearer to remind those who may not see education as important of the struggles that people of African descent endured to obtain an education equivalent to their white counterparts.

Preface

It is sad to say that we, descendants of slaves transported along the Middle Passage, have so much in common but know little about each other. We tend to remain comfortable in learning about history in our own countries but seldom come out of our comfort zone to gain information on the history of those African descendants who live outside of our countries. This has led to misconceptions and mistrust among us which is evident in the United States among African Americans and Black immigrants from other countries. But, many of these immigrants are often denied learning about their own history at schools in their countries. So, to those people, it may not seem logical to learn about another person's culture. Yet, in spite of the different languages and dialects, we have so many similarities. The only way to recognize each other with respect is through education and communication. *Beyond Educational Injustices* addresses one area of such commonality - through the educational system. Dr. William Gates has also recognized similarities in one of his documentaries that explores nations along the Middle Passage. It also highlights some countries where many in the United States had no idea that people of African descent existed. Furthermore, some may not be familiar that so many residents in Central America have continued to maintain their Jamaican and Caribbean heritage in language and culture that have been passed down from generation to generation. Writing this book will bring awareness to the educational experiences and connections of the population throughout so many countries that were impacted by the slave trade.

Beyond Educational Injustices also stems from a curiosity about my former secondary school. Throughout the years, it has been considered a prestigious school, so there is no wonder why many desire to be accepted into the institution. The current procedure to gain acceptance is competitive and stressful for those vying to attend. Parents may even spend more money than some can afford so that their children may take extra lessons to pass the standardized entrance exam to gain acceptance. The school maintains its popularity due to accomplishments in academics, sports, and ongoing ventures. The institution also continues to be lauded for its age-old existence and status for educating notable, successful alumni. Students are continuously reminded of the institution's rich history and highly-regarded benefactor. However, the school has an unspoken past of restricted enrollment policies during its inception in the 1800s at the height of slavery and after emancipation. The benefactor's possible connections to the sale and ownership of slaves also raise questions on the selective communications about the school's history. Nevertheless, for this and other early established schools with discriminatory enrollment histories, the population is now predominantly children of African descent. In contrast to praising the accomplishments of those age-old elitist institutions that were not established for the Black population, ***Beyond Educational Injustices*** lauds instead those schools that were opened primarily to serve the often-forgotten educational needs of the poor people of African descent and biracial populations.

Beyond Educational Injustices contains highlights of secondary and post-secondary institutions that were established for freed slaves and also during later years for their descendants in the United States, Caribbean, South and Central America. These institutions have greatly impacted the continued learning growth of a population who had otherwise been considered incapable of learning past the primary school level. The timeframe of establishment for those institutions range from during the slavery era to post emancipation to as recently as the 21st century. So, a number of students are now adjusting to having secondary schools which were not available to their parents and ancestors. Schools selected are located in capital cities or predominant minority populated communities or rural districts or coastal provinces or even in the deep forest of some countries. The book included secondary and post-secondary schools prior to the abolition of slavery in the United States. However, public schools catering to children of African descent prior to the abolition of slavery in other noted countries were non-existent. While there were public schools in those countries before the abolition of slavery, the institutions were established primarily to educate white children. Even after the abolition of slavery in some countries as outlined in the book, records show that children of African descent, upon completing elementary school, were not permitted to attend the earlier established schools since every possible policy was implemented to deny them admissions.

Readers should notice in the chapters' historic overviews each country's improper handling of the secondary and post-secondary educational needs of people of African heritage. Through the details, readers should surmise commonalities, despite geographic and language differences, among people residing in the noted countries. One similarity included how the white majority had forbidden slaves to learn to read and write and those caught breaking this law would be severely punished. The comparisons continue with injustices towards ex-slaves and their descendants in the denial of education well after the abolition of slavery. These ruling planters and merchants throughout the European colonies reluctantly adhered to the mandates of providing primary school education but did not waiver in their resistance to fund the construction of public schools that would address the secondary educational needs for students of African descent. Furthermore, the ruling class in the referenced countries denied the minority class the opportunity to attend existing private or even publicly funded secondary schools. Some churches in these countries were complicit in denying the rights of the Black population to continue their education since many denominational schools were established for whites only. Other religious-based schools accepted only a few biracial students from prominent families. Another similarity among slaves living in different countries was their earnest desire to become educated individuals since they knew the power of knowledge in providing a path to their freedom and/or upward mobility.

Readers may also identify differences in the book throughout the selected countries. For instance, with the exception of certain Central American countries, the Black population did not partake in opening their own elementary schools whereas in the United States, this minority class of people not only opened their own elementary schools but also secondary schools as well as universities prior to and after emancipation despite vocal oppositions, confrontations, and threats to their educational progress. So, unless monies came from trusts funds, or wealthy merchants, or denominational groups to build schools for their children, people of African descent and biracial residents in the former European colonies seemed to rely entirely on the colonial government to provide financial backings to build both elementary and secondary schools. Such a disadvantage meant that years and even a century after emancipation, millions were not educated past the elementary school level. They endured illiteracy and its consequences of poverty and unemployment from generation to generation

In some countries, descendants especially those living in deep rural communities are still waiting for secondary schools to be built so that they do not have to travel long distances or relocate elsewhere to obtain secondary education. In Venezuela, one would presume that communities with predominantly an Afro-Venezuelan population would, even today, not have any secondary schools if former president Hugo Chavez had not implemented the Bolivarian system that ensured the equality of education for the disenfranchised population. Even in Cuba, secondary education was not a government priority for the eastern provinces until after the revolution when the new government built secondary schools to meet the long-awaited needs of the largest Afro-Cuban population. Unfortunately, in other countries students of African descent are still prevented from exploring their true learning potentials and reaping accomplishments that could be achieved with continued education past the age of 14 years old.

Secondary and post-secondary schools noted in *Beyond Educational Injustices* include not only those where focus is placed on academics but also a variety of other types of school. For instance, in some countries learning at secondary schools has been adapted to a community's culture and/or the economic needs are incorporated into the educational output. This type of education is seen in vocational/technical high schools where subjects such as farming are a part of the curriculum. But even more surprising is that rare, age-old boarding high schools for those of African descent are still in operation with much determination despite many hardships. Also, other types of post-secondary institutions are discussed that include information on poly-technical schools, nursing schools, teachers' colleges, medical colleges, and military institutions.

Efforts are also made in ***Beyond Educational Injustices*** to highlight current problems that affect students. One problem in some of the former British colonies is the controlled enrollment of the Black population in secondary schools. Unbalanced placement of the brightest students continues to be made to the century-old secondary schools whose history may not have included the acceptance of the Black population. Students of lesser academic abilities are steered towards the "new" secondary schools that are often regarded as failing institutions. For South and Central America, current issues that were identified are that students from the minority Black population who reside in capital cities or other large urban areas have been transitioned into white majority secondary schools since the late 20th century. Such action has been to the detriment of their cultural upbringing that includes the loss of the native languages of their ancestors. The progress of those who reside in their own rural communities have been impacted by a governmental system of educational failures that have continued from generation to generation. The negative consequences of the state's control have often led to: neglect of frequent building maintenance, assignment of poorly trained teachers, and provision of limited funding for textbooks and other necessities that are expected to enhance students' learning. The frustrations for the lack of attention to schools located in areas where the primary enrollment are students of African descent have been shown by student and teachers' frequent demonstrations. Furthermore, although the Afro population residing in those cultural locations welcome the long-awaited secondary schools in their communities, sometimes the environment is not suitable, and it creates a negative impact that disrupts learning. The historic Black colleges and universities in the United States have also been experiencing their share of problems. A number of those historic Black institutions have been placed on warning, probation, or closed due to the decline in student enrollment, financial mismanagement, and administrative management issues.

Focus was placed on first introducing readers to the cities, towns, or communities where the noted secondary and post-secondary schools are located. This information should enable readers to become aware of the historical, social, and cultural impact associated with the noted institutions. Quite often, many of these communities are affected by poverty and high crime rates which ultimately impact the learning capacity of the children who reside in that volatile environment. Yet, many overcome the difficulties to graduate and progress onto post-secondary institutions.

For the most part, information gathered through research for *Beyond Educational Injustices* was readily available to provide an overview of the schools that have provided education to a marginalized population prior to and after the abolition of slavery. On the other hand, researched information was not readily available in some instances such as for the Afro-Cuban student populations at secondary and post-secondary institutions after Castro's revolution. Limited information on Afro-Cuban students also extended to locating records that associates connections with their community or participation in activities that promotes learning about their cultural.

Beyond Educational Injustices contains five chapters with information on secondary schools and post-secondary institutions that have impacted the lives of former slaves or their descendants. Countries selected are associated with regions along the Middle Passage where slaves were delivered. Those regions include the United States, the Caribbean, South and Central America. The population from these regions resides in countries where English or Spanish or French or Portuguese, or Dutch may be spoken.

North American Journey is dedicated entirely to schools in the United States that made a difference in educating slaves, ex-slaves, and their descendants. The chapter brings awareness to the tenacious efforts of African-Americans in developing their own high schools, colleges, and universities throughout the United States to educate a population that was denied entry into predominantly white-majority enrolled institutions. The chapter also includes reference to some of these notable high schools such as Paul Laurence Dunbar High School, and historically black colleges and universities (HBCU) such as Cheyney University.

British Caribbean Journey includes discussions on education in former British Caribbean territories. One such territory is Jamaica. According to Klein (1978), Jamaica received approximately 600,000 slaves, which was the highest intake of slaves in the British Caribbean region. Jamaica, Barbados, and a few other Caribbean countries take pride in the high schools that were established during the 17th and18th centuries. However, these high schools were not covered in detail in ***Beyond Educational Injustices*** since they were founded primarily to serve the ruling white population. Barbados's St. Leonard Boys Secondary School and Guyana's Community High Schools are two of the many secondary schools mentioned in this chapter. Trinidad and Tobago complete the list of countries identified in the chapter.

Suriname is generally aligned with the Caribbean versus South America where it is located, so the writings for this country was designated to the Other Caribbean Journey. Africans were brought to this Dutch Caribbean territory where their descendants, too, experienced difficulties in obtaining secondary education after the abolition of slavery and were impacted for generations thereafter. Since slavery in the Caribbean was also affected by Spanish influences, the learning experiences of slaves and former slaves in Cuba were explored in the Other Caribbean Journey. Many Afro-Cuban descendants remain in coastal areas such as Santiago de Cuba, so a high school was selected from the area. Haiti was the first colony to obtain independence with its slavery intake of 450,000 by 1787 (Arsenault, Lozano, et al, 2006). It was important to investigate the learning experiences of slaves, ex-slaves, and their descendants in this former French territory and explore the schools that were opened to serve the Afro-Haitian majority population.

Brazil was the major recipient of the slave trade with 4,000,000 slaves. As a result, included in South American Journey is the country's history of denying secondary education to Afro-Brazilians after emancipation. The Afro-Brazilian population waited centuries after the abolition of slavery for secondary schools, such as Colegio Estadual Journalist Tim Lopes, to be built in communities where poverty and violence affect the learning of students. Colombia has the second largest Afro-Latino population in South America. So, Colombia was included in this chapter. Since the country was greatly influenced by the slave trade, ***Beyond Educational Injustices*** contains facts on the state's reactions towards the learning needs of Afro-Colombians. Further, the chapter explains how the lengthy civil war suspended the education of children residing in the dense forest that was also home to their ancestors during the slavery era. Venezuela rounds off this chapter, and it contains the history of education for Afro-Venezuelans from the slavery era to now under former President Hugo Chavez's Bolivarian educational system.

Central American was also affected by the Trans-Atlantic slave trade, so Nicaragua with its large Afro-Nicaraguan population, primarily descendants of West Indian immigrants, was discussed in Central American Journey. Readers will learn how the education of the population was compromised during the earlier years, and it was further impacted when many were displaced as a result of the civil war which was fought mainly throughout the coastal wooded lands where Afro-Nicaraguans have occupied. The divisions between descendants of early African settlers and West Indian immigrant workers were also explained in Central American Journey. Afro-Costa Ricans of Jamaican heritage, their experiences of apartheid, and their refusal to give up their English language in favor of Spanish are mentioned in the chapter since the early education of these immigrants were at English language schools.

The author hopes that ***Beyond Educational Injustices*** will shed light on the post-secondary schools and tertiary institutions that have made a difference in educating majority of people who otherwise were considered as not having the capability to learn past the elementary school level. It is also expected that the book will provide knowledge that the struggles in educating African descendants have continued centuries after the abolition of slavery throughout countries where slaves were transported. The author wishes that readers of this book are not only those whose countries are mentioned in the book but others so that they too will become knowledgeable of the history of post-secondary and tertiary schooling or the lack thereof for ex-slaves and their descendants throughout the centuries.

Introduction

A Crime to Educate Slaves in the United States

The first African free school was opened in New York City in 1787 (Spartacus Educational, n.d.) and other northern schools were opened thereafter to educate those of color whose movements were unrestricted. However, throughout the southern states, laws were passed forbidding slaves from learning to read and write. So, during the 18th century there were no known schools in the southern states of America that admitted slaves into their free public schools. Slaves were considered property, not as human beings who should be educated. Furthermore, slave owners feared that an educated slave could be a threat to them and their livelihood. Most owners believed that teaching slaves was dangerous since it would make them difficult to control and likely to run away or cause rebellion. As a result, most white slaveholders were adamant that slaves should not be educated due to their fear of threats to their authority by an educated slave population.

Throughout the south, a number of statutes were enacted to criminalize persons who were caught teaching slaves or supporting any efforts to teach them. For example, North Carolina's 1830 statute included that "any free person, who shall hereafter teach, or attempt to teach, any slave within this State to read or write, the use of figures excepted, or shall give or sell to such slave or slaves any books or pamphlets, shall be liable to indictment in any court of record in this State." (Williams, 2005). In 1740 South Carolina passed the following legislation: "Whereas, the having slaves taught to write, or suffering them to be employed in writing, may be attended with great

"

inconveniences; Be it enacted, that all and every person and persons whatsoever, who shall hereafter teach or cause any slave or slaves to be taught to write, or shall use or employ any slave as a scribe, in any manner of writing whatsoever, hereafter taught to write, every such person or persons shall, for every such offense, forfeit the sum of one hundred pounds, current money." (Simkin, 2015).

White teachers who were discovered educating slaves would be run out of town. Margaret Douglass, who was caught teaching slaves in Norfolk, Virginia, was convicted and imprisoned for her actions (Simkin, 2015). Simkin (2015) wrote that Henry Bibb, a slave in Shelby County, Kentucky, recalled in his autobiography, *Narrative of the Life and Adventures of Henry Bibb, An American Slave*: "Slaves were not allowed books, pen, ink, nor paper, to improve their minds. There was a Miss Davies, a poor white girl, who offered to teach a Sabbath School for the slaves. Books were supplied and she started the school; but the news got to our owners that she was teaching us to read. This caused quite an excitement in the neighborhood. Patrols were appointed to go and break it up the next Sabbath." In Virginia in 1841, the punishment for breaking such a law was 20 lashes with a whip to the slave and a fine of $100 to the teacher. In North Carolina in 1841, punishment consisted of 39 lashes to the slave and a fine of $250 to the teacher. Education was not illegal in Kentucky, but it was virtually nonexistent. Missouri was an exception because some slaveholders educated their slaves or permitted the slaves to educate themselves.

In other states, however, severe physical and psychological punishment would be administered to those slaves who were caught educating themselves. For those states with restrictions, some of the physical and psychological punishments to slaves included not only savage whippings but also torture, amputation of fingers and toes, or even death. Nevertheless, slaves took the risks since occasionally, literacy was the driving force that afforded their escape to freedom. For those who had not obtained physical freedom, developing an ability to read and write meant intellectual freedom. Through such knowledge, some, such as Frederick Douglas and Harriet Jacobs, wrote slave narratives. These narratives uncovered to the world the brutality that slaves suffered at the hands of their white owners.

After emancipation, a gracious reception was not always received for all schools opened for freed students in some northern states. For instance, when Prudence Crandall, a Quaker, opened a school for freed girls in Canterbury, Connecticut, angry whites made all attempts to burn down the building. The failed attempt prompted others to prevent the school from receiving essential supplies. However, the school continued to attract girls from other cities such as Philadelphia and Boston. Further efforts were made to close down the school when local authorities used a vagrancy law against students that would cause them to receive ten whip lashes for attending school. The law was overturned with the support of the Anti-Slavery Society. Simkin (2015) reports a later change in attitude after public education was extended to Boston in 1855 when the Massachusetts Legislature changed its policy of rejecting students of African descent and declared that "no person shall be excluded from a Public School on account of race, color or prejudice."

European Colonies -
Education During Slavery and the Colonial Era

A French Colonial governor of Martinique wrote to a French minister in Haiti during the late 1700s stating, "The safety of the whites demands that we keep the Negroes in the most profound ignorance. I have reached the stage of believing firmly that one must treat the Negroes as one treats beasts" (Pamphile, 2008). In addition to their fear of revolts, the ruling white class's general belief was that Africans lacked intellectual qualities and the potential for "progress and perfectibility." Montesquieu, the great philosopher of the Enlightenment, who made humor of slavery, sarcastically insinuated to his peers that the people of Africa lacked superior faculties, their cognitive abilities would not project any measurable knowledge, and therefore it was impossible to teach them anything.

During the 17th and 18th centuries, all efforts were made by wealthy planters to establish education foundations by bequeathing property and fund to start schools for both poor white children and biracial children, classified as white, who could not afford private instruction or to migrate to England and France to continue their studies. Schools located in the British colonies that were established for those children included Codrington College and Harrison College in Barbados and Wolmer's, Rusea's, Beckford and Smith's, and Manning's schools in Jamaica (Global Foundation to Upgrade Underserved Primary and Secondary Schools, n.d.) Throughout the colonial territories, slaves were not allowed to read and write because the majority of slave-owners were opposed to any suggestions to educate their slaves. So, there was no action taken to provide a formal system of education for slaves. When the first missionaries arrived in the Caribbean during the mid-18th century, a number of non-conformist preachers provided slaves with instruction in the doctrines of Christianity in spite of opposition from slave owners. Missionaries eventually upgraded their teachings to include Bible instruction. This change alarmed owners because they believed Bible instructions would include learning to read and write. In countries such as Barbados where laws existed that did not forbid teaching slaves to read and write, an Act in 1797 was passed that it was the duty of every Anglican priest to try to convert the slaves. However, this act made it illegal to teach them to read and write. Some slaves ignored the law and continued with their quest to be educated. Nevertheless, right up until the end of slavery, elementary education was not provided to slaves.

Slave children under six years of age were emancipated in 1834 while full emancipation was extended to all children in 1838 at which time the British colony was expected to provide a public education system for the former slaves. Ex-slave masters continued to maintain their overall view that educating African descendants would make them unfit or unwilling to continue their customary manual labor. But, the reforming government in England held conflicting perceptions that the educational fulfillment of the majority population would bring peace and prosperity to the empire. Furthermore, the empire stuck with the belief that emancipation had removed the controls of the working class and in order to avoid destabilization of the Caribbean society, education could avert any impending disruptions thereby maintaining the dominance of the white landowners. Eventually, planters realized that educating slaves could be beneficial to them by serving as a means to check their movements (King, 1998). Therefore, the public elementary education system was established throughout the British Caribbean as a means to control the emancipated slaves. During that period, students were taught Christian education to maintain their subservient behavior to the plantocracy.

Secondary education was considered "the education of the middle class to keep pace with that obtained by the laboring class in the elementary schools" ((King, 1998). "Secondary education was regarded as education of a higher grade among those classes of the community who would value it if placed within their reach, but whose means do not enable them to send their children to Europe for the purpose of receiving it" (King, 1998). This post-elementary education was considered in the colonial territories as a means of upward mobility for the white middle class and poor residing on the lands of European territories. It was never intended for emancipated children to attend secondary schools, so the elementary and secondary systems were designed to be entirely separated. According to King (1988) the norm was to implement inferior education at elementary schools and superior education at the secondary schools. For example, in 1891 in Barbados, the government spent two-thirds of funds allocated for education on approximately 600 whites and students passing as white who were attending secondary schools while the remaining one-third was assigned to elementary schools with a population of approximately 23,000 students from Black working class families.

The North American Journey

United States
Education During and After Slavery

Slavery in the United States began in the 1600 when approximately 20 Africans were transported to Jamestown, Virginia. The number of slaves grew rapidly as white settlers began to rely on cheaper labor. Up to the 18th century, slaves worked on tobacco, rice, and indigo plantations from the northern state of Maryland to the southern state of Georgia. During the 18th century, the mechanization of the textile industry in England created a demand for cotton in the United States. By that time, tobacco production was exhausted, so those plantations were converted to produce the well sought-after cotton throughout southern states. By the time Congress outlawed the slave trade in 1808, approximately 390,000 had been shipped to the United States. It was not until 1862 that President Lincoln signed a preliminary emancipation proclamation which became official in 1863. The proclamation did not end slave which persisted until 1865 on the passage of the 13th Amendment after the end of the Civil War. Throughout the American south during slavery, planters hired tutors to educate their children or sent them to private schools, sometimes in northern states and even in Europe. However, a need to educate children was not extended to slaves who would be severely punished if they were caught simply reading and writing. Nevertheless, threats of harsh consequences did not prevent slaves' continued thirst for learning by devising resourceful tactics. Some brave white teachers such as John Chavis in Raleigh, North Carolina, ran secret night schools. According to Williams (2005) some slaves were educated in "pit schools" that got the name from the pit(s) in the ground located deep in the distant woods out of their master's reach. Slaves would also hide spelling books under their hats so the reading materials could be readily available

whenever they encountered a literate person who they
could trust or bribe to teach them. Even the Civil War did
not deter a slave's desire to become educated, and this is
evidenced by the commitment of those dedicated soldiers
who completed their lessons during their lunch breaks.
Williams (2015) also acknowledges that during the
transition from slavery to emancipation, schooling was just
as important as their material needs.

In some northern and mid-western states, schools, such as
Philadelphia's Institute for Colored Youth - also known as
Cheyney University - were established for freed persons to
attend prior to the Civil War. Some schools were also
started in union occupied southern territories during the
Civil War, but a multitude of schools were erected once
slavery was abolished in an effort to meet freed adult and
children's high demand for education. These schools were
supported by the Freedmen's Bureau, northern White
charities, and missionary societies. Communities, even
those where the very poor resided, made all effort to
provide whatever resources they could to build and
maintain their schools. Many of the schools started in
homes and church basements or old school buildings. In
addition, a great desire to learn encouraged fund-raisings,
donations of land, and the use of volunteers' manual labor
to establish thousands of new schools throughout the south.
The former slaves would unite and pool their meagre funds
to build and operate their own schools. Some attended these
schools by walking long distances, dressed in tattered
clothes with no shoes. They were determined to spend long
days inside the classroom with less vacation days so they
could get the most out of education and eventually use their
knowledge to become teachers and advocates for their
communities. Ironically, one slave school, the Savannah
Slave Market School, was established in the building where
slaves were sold thereby separating families. There were

elementary and secondary day schools, night schools, and Sabbath schools. Many of these schools did not have formal names because they were not operating under an established school system.

The Freedmen's Bureau, the government established entity, became involved in the complex task of rapidly developing schools throughout the southern states. The bureau not only paid monthly tuition fees but also raised monies for teachers' room and board, purchased plots of land for school houses, donated building materials, and secured labor to complete the job. They also created and supported schools without the independent support of northern entities (Butchart, 2002). One of their early schools was The Chimborazo School in Richmond, Virginia which was founded in 1865. The Freedmen Bureau managed to secure the premises of the Confederate hospital for the school. The school's register indicates that students ranged from four years old to 29 years old. James Plantation School, another freedman school, was opened to children living in North Carolina. In addition to schools opened by the Freedmen Bureau, other schools included Mary Battey's who created classes for freed slaves in Andersonville, Georgia. Battey wrote in 1866 that in spite of threats from the white community, 27 Black students attended on the first day of school. The enrollment increased six weeks later to 85 students. Battey expressed that over a seven-year period of teaching these students, they demonstrated their eagerness to learn regardless of the long distances they had to travel back and forth to school (Simkin, 2015).

A handful of private northern missionary organizations began to enroll freed persons into their basic education institutions prior to the abolition of slavery, while other northern denominations increased opportunities by establishing colleges for them. After emancipation, the Northern Missionary Associations forged into the south to establish private schools that would address the need for secondary education. For instance, in 1865, the American Missionary Association was instrumental in founding the Fisk School and a number of other southern Black colleges. Since the population comprised of mainly low-income students, tuition was kept at a minimum while the church assumed most of the financial obligations and subsidized the salary of some teachers. Church-based schools throughout the south increased in the 1900s to 250 schools with an enrollment close to 45,000 students.

The academy school was a groundbreaking type of institution established to admit freed slaves and others during the post-civil war era (Ruelas, 2017). The regimented day school or boarding school was an innovative concept that provided students with academic subjects such as reading, writing, and mathematics along with extra-curriculum activities that included cooking, sewing, and domestic arts to balance the educational experiences of students. The initial intentions of the schools were to provide students with basic literacy so they could read the Bible, complete basic math calculations, and understand labor contracts. But white teachers brought a liberal arts curriculum to the schools which was later continued by teachers of African descent who took over instructions. Later, industrial arts courses were included

The passage of the Second Morrill Act in 1890 required states with racially segregated public higher education systems to open public land-grant institutions primarily for students of African descent. A number of Black colleges were sponsored by their states to be considered in the land-grant program where institutions would be designated as agricultural colleges and entitled to receive federal funding for their agricultural and industrial programs. Black colleges included Tuskegee Normal School for Colored Teachers and Hampton Normal and Agricultural Institute.

Both set the standards of offering industrial education. The act also opened the door for the establishment of institutions such as Florida A & M University and 15 other Black colleges that were designated as land-grant colleges. While most offered courses in agricultural, mechanical, and industrial subjects, few provided students with college-level courses and degrees. In spite of the many achievements accomplished in educating freed persons after emancipation, the racist structure overshadowed the successes after the end of Reconstruction (Ruelas, 2017).

Up until the 1960s, centuries after the abolition of slavery, schools remained segregated throughout southern states even though in 1954 the Supreme Court in Brown versus the Board of Education landmark case overturned state laws by ruling that separate schools for children based on race were unconstitutional. The Little Rock Nine is a famous instance that showed white resistance to the Supreme Court's ruling since a group of Black students were heckled, spat upon, and denied entry on the first day that they had been expected to desegregate Central High School in Little Rock, Arkansas, in September 1957. Also, in the case of the University of Alabama, two Afro-Americans who wanted to enroll in the institution in 1963 were blocked from entering the enrollment office by the then governor and state troopers. Nevertheless, the next day, the governor yielded under pressure from the federal government to allow both students to enroll at the university.

Historically Black Colleges and Universities (HBCU) represent the schools remaining today from the institutions that were established in northern and mid-western states prior to the Civil War and those that were founded throughout the deep south to educate African Americans after the Civil War. They were founded primarily to educate former slaves and those born as freed people who were denied admission to white colleges and universities. Therefore, HBCUs were founded due to a need to provide post-secondary education to those who desired to continue their education. The first HBCU was Institute for Colored Youth now known as Cheyney University – 1837, and others thereafter were: Lincoln University – 1854; Wilberforce University – 1856; Harris-Stowe State College – 1857; Bowie State University – 1856; and LeMoyne-Owen College 1862. Although these institutions were known as universities, the primary mission during the early years was to provide elementary and secondary schooling for those who had no previous education. Their offerings changed during the early 1900s when higher level post-secondary courses and programs were provided. Teacher training was later an important focus of the HBCU so as to meet the need of the large growth of students attending secondary schools. The U.S. Department of Education (1991) reports that by 1953, more than 32,000 students were enrolled in such well known private Black institutions as Fisk University, Hampton Institute, Howard University, Meharry Medical College, Morehouse College, Spelman College, and Tuskegee Institute. Others attended smaller Black colleges located throughout southern and bordered states. During that same year, over 43,000 students were enrolled in public Black colleges with 3,200 students enrolled in graduate programs.

Many of the HBCUs still remain open after 150 years. However, according to Jacobs (2015), a number of these colleges and universities are struggling financially and even on the verge of financial collapse. The financial problems have arisen from unequal government funding, declining enrollment, and poor leadership. Plus, the recession at the end of 2010 contributed to the problems. However, one of the trends is the rapid desegregation of many of the public and state funded HBCUs. For instance, West Virginia State

University, which began as a historically Black institution, has currently a majority white student body. This trend is expected to persist in HBCU institutions where the growth of the white student population exceeds that of the Afro-American population in the surrounding cities or states. Also, D. Coleman (n.d.) mentions that competing with white schools is challenging because these schools can afford to provide students with dormitories having high-speed internet connections, cable TV, microwaves, and suites with kitchens and private bathrooms whereas the HBCUs cannot afford to provide attractive amenities that are customary also to Afro-American students (Coleman, n.d.) Nevertheless, many high school students still prefer to attend a HBCU that is known for producing graduates who have achieved successful careers.

Washington D.C.

Washington D.C. was an active and profitable slave depot prior to the Civil War (George Mason University, n.d.). The booming business was significantly apparent around the U.S. Capitol and White House as groups of chained slaves passed these government buildings daily. Slave pens were scattered around the National Mall during the early 1800. Slaves were kept under inhumane conditions in these pens and also cells while they awaited their sale and relocation. Hotel and taverns not far from the Capitol were sites of slave auctions. Basement rooms were rented in hotels around the Mall so that newly-purchased slaves could be kept before they were taken to their destinations throughout the U.S. Slavery's presence, especially in the capital of a nation, brought recognition to the hypocrisy of the ideal that "all men are created equal". After decades of controversy, the Compromise of 1850 abolished the slave trade in Washington D.C. In 1862, the District of Columbia Emancipation Act freed all enslaved people in Washington D.C. thereby ending decades of what abolitionists called "the national shame." (George Mason University, n.d.)

During the Civil War and the Reconstruction era, more than 25,000 African Americans moved to Washington D.C. because it was primarily pro-Union and as the nation's capital, this made it a popular city to reside. By 1900, Washington had the largest percentage of African Americans of any city in the nation because of opportunities for federal jobs. Another reason for moving to Washington D.C. was the high standards of education that was available to Blacks in the city. Students attended schools such as The Preparatory School for Colored Youth, the city's first public high school. Howard University was a magnet for professors and post-secondary students. Furthermore, African American men gained the right to vote in Washington D.C. as a result of the passage of Congress's Reconstruction Act of 1867. This act was three years prior to the passage of the 15th Amendment that granted all African-American men throughout the United States the right to vote.

African American residents participated in riots and passive resistance against racist practices during the Jim Crow and Civil Rights eras. The activism ultimately led by 1975 to further increase in the city's population to represent 70 percent of the residents (McQuirter, 2003). The population has gone through challenges in their communities throughout the years which include the effects from poverty and crime. However, they have maintained their political and cultural dominance during the years with the election of mayors and congress members. In addition, African-Americans are involved in different movements, the arts, independent think tanks, schools, and other entities that cater to their race.

Paul Laurence Dunbar High School

Paul Laurence Dunbar High School was the first public high school for freed persons since efforts to integrate traditional public high schools throughout Washington D.C. failed. Originally named the Preparatory High School for Colored Youth, the institution was started as a prep school in a basement of a church with four students in 1870. The student population increased steadily throughout the years. Paul Laurence Dunbar High School provided students with an excellent academic curriculum, and its college-tract offerings attracted many parents who moved to Washington DC so that their children would obtain this well-sought after education in subjects such as English, Latin, foreign languages, history, and mathematics. As a result, the school produced many graduates with prestigious careers. Some alumni returned to teach at the school after graduating from colleges and universities. In fact, the teachers and principals were well qualified since some possessed Ph. D.s and advanced degrees (Bonner, Freelain, Henderson, et. al 2011). Throughout the years, as enrollment increased, the school changed its location a number of times. When it moved to its M Street address in 1891, the school was known as the M Street High School. It was renamed in 1916 in honor of the Afro-American poet Paul Laurence Dunbar when the school was relocated to its present address on N Street.

Even today, Paul Laurence Dunbar High School continues to attract a predominantly African-American population. However, its prestigious status changed. After the integration of high schools in Washington DC and Paul Laurence Dunbar High School's failure to do so, it lost its elite status since its government funding decreased. So, by the 1960s, the school was affected by teacher shortages, insufficient classroom space, poor maintenance causing the buildings to deteriorate, and inadequate athletic facilities. It became a community school and could no longer accept students who did not reside in the neighborhood. This led to an enrolment of students from the surrounding low-income community with lower learning abilities. Producing failing grades in reading and mathematics, the high school began experiencing a decline in student achievement with decreased graduation rates that impacted its previous stellar reputation. Notwithstanding, in 2013, students began to experience learning in a brand-new building with state-of-the-art classrooms and sports facilities along with electronic equipment. The new school also includes a college type atmosphere with a four-story academy wing containing a museum, kitchen and cafeteria, library and media center, a health clinic as well as a dental suite, auditorium theater space, gymnasium and swimming pool, a student services center, and a child care center (Spinell, 2013). Since 2015, the school has increased their graduation rate with double digit gains. In spite of the graduation increases, as of this writing, the rate of college bound students has not reached the high level it did during the school's successful past.

Missouri
St. Louis

The African race was a part of St. Louis since the first European settlement in 1764 (National Park Service, 2015). When the United States assumed political control of St. Louis in 1804, life changed for slaves who had lived under the French and Spanish systems. So-called "black laws" were written which added far more restrictive regulations to slave life. The city became a major slave auctioning center. The National Park Service (2015) report indicates that by 1850, St. Louis had become a rapidly-growing city of over 80,000 residents including 2,656 slaves. The free persons of color numbered 1,398. While some were prominent landowners and craftsmen, a few were the wealthiest citizens of the city. As the number of immigrants increased and the slave count remained stable, slavery became unprofitable. Slaves hired themselves out to earn money for their owners. Their work away from the plantations enabled them to keep some or all of these wages plus work on Sundays and holidays to earn extra money. A very small number were set free by masters. Other slaves managed to save enough money to purchase their own freedom. Another small number of slaves sued for their freedom in St. Louis courts based on the presumption that they had been held as slaves for a period of time in a free state.

During the great migration after Reconstruction, many former slaves from the rural south moved to St. Louis. Their relocation continued to increase steadily up until 1910 since they were lured by factory jobs at developing industrial centers. However, today, Black residents are leaving St. Louis in greater number, according to the 2017 estimates from the U.S. Census Bureau (Edgell, 2018). The statistics show more than 4,000 African American residents select to move elsewhere to communities that can provide them with a better working opportunities and quality of life which includes improved access to schools and other resources.

Charles Sumner High School

Charles Sumner High School was established due to the adoption of the Constitution of 1865 in Missouri, which required that regional school boards support the education of free slave children in their districts (Clio, n.d.). The institution opened its doors in 1875 as the first public high school for the population living in St. Louis and on the western side of the Mississippi River. It was initially named the High School for Colored Students during the Reconstruction era but later was renamed after the Massachusetts abolitionist Senator Charles Sumner who dedicated part of his life to the equality and freedom of his people. The public institution was welcomed because many previous attempts to start a school failed shortly after their inception. For example, T.S. Eliot co-founded a school to educate free and escaped slaves, but two days after opening, it was burned down. Charles Sumner High School went through two location changes, and the first occurred when parents successfully lobbied for the move from the downtown St. Louis location since they did not want their children to walk past the gallows and city morgue. The school was moved a second time because parents did not think it was appropriate for the school to be located in close proximity to saloons and pool houses where children had to pass. The institution has been at its present location since 1908 at Ville where a large African-American population has resided. In spite of the steady growth of the African-American population in Ville, Charles Sumner High School remained the only all public high school for many years until 1927 when Vashon High School was founded.

Today, Charles Sumner High School still has an enrollment of predominantly African-American students. However, according to Crouch, (2015), the prosperity of Ville has been affected over the decades because the African-American middle-class residents of the area have moved to other parts of the city and to the suburbs. In the suburbs, parents have been enrolling their children in better-funded schools. So, with the migration of the middle-class families and the deterioration of Charles Sumner High School, enrollment has declined. Many students have opted to attend other high schools such as the nearby Soldan-Blewett High School which was located much closer to those who had previously been forced to travel further for school primarily because of their race. In addition, by the 2000s, students had the option of choosing magnet schools and charter schools.

Charles Sumner High School's academic performance has deteriorated to become one of the worst in the school district. In addition, violence has overtaken the campus because students today are more than likely to reside in impoverished homes and may be burdened with emotional and social needs (Crouch, 2015). In 2009, the school district's Superintendent made a petition to close the institution. However, after meeting with the alumni, they made a commitment to address the problems by getting parents involved, mentoring students, and volunteering at events. Since 2009, graduation rates have improved. However, the current improvements are still not satisfactory by state standards and, with continued decline in enrollment, the school remains one of the lowest performing schools in the district as of this writing. But stakeholders continue to make proposals on revamping academic offerings in an effort to improve student achievement.

Mississippi
Piney Woods

The Rankin County Piney Woods region in Mississippi was regarded as having the poorest land, cattle, and people. (Harrison, 1982). Harrison (1982) also explained that the area was primarily settled by whites from the Carolinas and Georgia who could not afford to purchase land in the delta. In addition, former slaves occupied the land for similar reasons - its cheapness. During the 1900 and 1910 census, African Americans comprised more than 58 percent of the county's population. Of the 2,802 African American males of voting age, 51 percent were illiterate (Bureau of Census, 1910). This illiteracy provided white land owners with a labor force presumed to be ignorant, docile, and dependent upon whites. So, with a lack of education, the constant threats of lynching, and the restrictions of "separate but equal" laws, African Americans in Piney Woods, as with those in other parts of Mississippi, were repressed socially, politically, and economically. Feelings of hope for their children and future generations finally came to the disenfranchised people of Piney Woods in 1909 when the Piney Woods Country Life School was opened. This school has remained a symbol in the community where children of African descent can obtain a high standard of secondary education.

Piney Woods Country Life School

Piney Woods Country Life School is one of the few remaining historic boarding schools that have a predominant African-American student population. The school was opened in 1909 by Dr. Laurence Jones who realized a need to start a high school to educate poor children not only to read and write but also to focus on practical and industrial programs such as farming. Opening the school with only $2 in his pocket on land donated by a former slave, this task was not easy for Dr. Jones and his wife who had to deal with the threats of lynching and even the governor of Mississippi who was considered a white supremacist. Furthermore, the poverty-stricken status of the population was another factor that was expected to threaten regular attendance of those enrolled. However, they persisted against the odds and kept the school open by cleverly collaborating with white business owners in the county. This strategy not only enabled the school to receive assistance from those who would otherwise object to its existence, but the mutual friendships also guaranteed the school's security. Dr. Jones received lumber and other resources to build the school that would provide the community with better educated workers. Student enrollment increased steadily, and the community continued to give whatever they could from a few dollars or even pennies to labor. In 1910, the property was deeded to the trustees of the school and three years later a charter was granted to the institution that became known as the Piney Woods Country Life School.

During the Great Recession, the small, historic boarding school struggled to maintain funding from its private donations and foundations. The school subsequently had to cut back in its student enrollment when its endowment was affected by the steep decline in the stock market. So, its 500-student population declined. Today enrollment has increased, and the school has maintained this steady admission of students in grades 9 to 12.

The 60-acre school, located in the wooded hillside, is considered the largest historically Black boarding school out of the few remaining. The school's earlier academic offerings of vocational and agriculture classes have been upgraded to a rigorous college prep program. The demanding curriculum has placed a high expectation on students who are all required to graduate and attend college. Campbell (2015) mentioned that some 97 percent of students who graduated in 2014 earned college acceptances to attend various colleges all over the country. Students are not only natives of the surrounding communities and elsewhere in Mississippi, but they come from different states and even other parts of the world such as the African continent and the Caribbean. For the most part, all students receive tuition assistance or a scholarship to help cover the approximately $23,000 annual cost. For this financial benefit, they must enroll in the work-study program for part-time employment on-campus. The campus is self-sufficient with its own post office, farm, athletic fields, chapel, and amphitheater.

Pennsylvania
Thornbury Township

Thornbury Township, in rural Pennsylvania, was known as a tolerant community since it was influenced partly by the lenient disposition of the Quakers, the earlier settlers. The accepting temperament made it possible for African Americans to prosper in the township much earlier than those who lived in other areas throughout the United States. As a result, Thornbury African Methodist Church was established in 1834; a Black judge was elected in the late 1800s; and the Institute for Colored Youth, now known as Cheyney University of Pennsylvania, was relocated to the Cheyney Farm in 1902. In addition, the House of Refuge, founded in 1828 for court-referred young men throughout the country, was relocated to Thornbury Township in 1892.

Thornbury was a predominant farming community during earlier years. However, housing and commercial construction expanded throughout the 20th century, especially after World War II. The growing community required more infrastructure and that included the addition of a post office in Cheyney.

Cheyney University

Cheyney University, established on February 25, 1837, is the first institution of higher learning for African Americans. It was founded as a school for teacher education before Abraham Lincoln signed the Emancipation Proclamation. The university was known initially as the Institute for Colored Youth and located in Philadelphia. Prior to changing its name to Cheyney University, the school was relocated to the rural town of Cheyney, Pennsylvania. The institution was a $10,000 bequest of Richard Humphreys, a Quaker philanthropist.

He wanted one tenth of his estate to be used to design and establish a school to educate the descendants of the African race. A native of Tortola, West Indies, he was appalled on coming to the United States in 1764 to witness the struggles of freed persons who faced difficulties in securing jobs due to the influx of immigrants. After the race riot in Philadelphia in 1764, Humphrey decided to write his will that specifically instructed 13 fellow Quakers to design an institution "...to instruct the descendants of the African race in school learning, in the various branches of the mechanic arts, trades and agriculture, in order to prepare and fit and qualify them to act as teachers...." (Cheyney University, n.d.). While the name of this rural institution has changed a number of times throughout the years, the vision of providing quality instruction remains the same.

K. Woodhouse (2015) wrote that the institution is now facing many struggles. Building infrastructure was reported as deteriorating. But, another major issue for the school has been its financial difficulties. This indicates the university has expenses exceeding revenues and increasing uncollectible debt. In fact, the 2016 deficit was 45 million as a result of the decreasing enrollment and government underfunding. These issues have caused a great decrease in enrollment. Since the school has no financial reserves or endowment to offset the problems, it began to recruit students representing a variety of races, cultures, and nationalities. But it has continued to experience a steep decline in students with a 31-year low in spite of 700 in 2016. During that same year, a group of supporters, *Heeding Cheyney's Call*, filed a civil rights law suit against the Pennsylvania State System of Higher Education (PASSHE) alleging decades of discrimination in funding. At the end of 2015, the institution was placed on probation due to financial concerns uncovered by the associations that accredit colleges and universities. It was given two years to correct the issues or face losing accreditation (Associated Press, 2015). This means students would not be entitled to receive state or federal financial aid. No doubt with increased funding from PASSHE, the school should be able to turn its declining status around in order to avoid the closing of this historic institution.

Oxford Township

Oxford Township, known previously as Hood's Township, was founded in 1754. The area was split into Upper and Lower Oxford Townships in 1797. The township is in Chester County which previously had a large slave population. The slave register of 1780 includes information that there were 142 slaveholders in Chester County alone and a total of 470 slaves (Kashatus, 2002). The number of slaveholders appears excessive. But, probate records for eastern Chester County and the tax lists for the entire Chester County indicate a much smaller percentage of rural inhabitants owned slaves in comparison to those slaveholders in Philadelphia prior to 1770. Many of the slaves came directly from the West Indies because slaves coming from Africa did not adapt well to working in the cold climate. The price of a slave during the mid-17th century was from 40 pounds to 100 pounds (Futhey and Cope 1881). Since this amount of money was considerable, the need for slaves to acclimatize quickly to the weather was economically beneficial to slave owners. However, in spite of the demand for slaves in Chester County, some groups tried to discourage the immoral practice. The Society of Friends made all effort to dissuade its members from participating in the slave trade in Chester County (Futhey and Cope 1881). So, abolitionists passed out flyers discouraging slavery. Another tactic in Chester County was to boycott goods made by slaves which would have not only impacted the slave owner but those merchants selling the products. Nevertheless, the efforts made in the slaves' favor did not prevent some of them from escaping the daily cruelties especially because the area became an important connection to the Underground Railroad. Runaway slaves were guided to freedom via Chester County and other secret, illegal route throughout the country. While slavery continued, opportunities materialized in 1854 for freed persons when Lincoln University was opened in the eastern part of Lower Oxford Township. This opening provided learning opportunities for those who were denied enrollment into post-secondary institutions for white students only.

All children enrolled from elementary through high school in Oxford Township attended classes in a new school building opened in 1905, except for African-American children. They continued to be taught separately from white students in an old building. Furthermore, their learning was reduced from grades one through eight. Racial segregation of students continued in Oxford Township until late 1940s.

The 2010 census for the township indicates a 35.1 percent Black population. Students at Lincoln University are represented in this population of African descent in the Lower Oxford Township. These residents stood up for their rights as a result of their experiences of election biases in 2008. In so doing, Lincoln University students and Chester County residents filed a Federal lawsuit alleging that the Chester County Board of Elections and Department of Voter Services deprived African-Americans in Lower Oxford Township of their right to vote by assigning them to inconvenient and inadequate polling facilities on Election Day, 2008 (ALCU, 2010). On that day, voters, primarily African Americans residing in Lower Oxford East, waited up to seven hours in the pouring rain to cast their votes. Many became frustrated with the long wait time and left without casting their votes. One condition of the settlement was to return the Lower Oxford East polling station to the Lincoln University campus where it had been housed during the 1990s.

Lincoln University

Lincoln University was founded as a private university in 1854 and established as the country's first degree granting Black institution. John Miller Dickey and his wife Sarah Emlen Cresson founded the institution because of the difficulties Dickey encountered in gaining college admissions for a freedman and the difficulties he observed by other free persons in gaining acceptance to even the most liberal universities. Originally named the Ashmun Institute, the school was renamed Lincoln University in 1866 in honor of President Abraham Lincoln. From as early as such time, Dickie, the first president of the university, made known his intentions to enroll a diverse student male population, and this expectation was followed up throughout the years with the enrollment of students not only throughout the United States but also from countries around the world including the African continent. During those early years, the school was favorably considered as 'the Black Princeton' because of its university educated founder, faculty, and the extensive classical curriculum. An African-American president of the college was not conferred until 1945 when its 1923 graduate, Horace Mann Bond, became the 8th leader. In 1953, the institution became co-educational when the charter was amended to permit women to enroll in degreed programs.

The school continues to attract a variety of students from all over the world. The university campus houses costly, modern facilities such as the Ivory V. Nelson Center for the Sciences, the International Cultural Center, the Health and

29

Wellness Center, the renovated Student Union building and
Langston Hughes Library. The students also are provided
with technology enhanced classrooms. Lincoln University's
dual enrollment program with Coatesville Area High
School enables those students to earn college credit by
taking classes at the high school during their regular school
hours.

Georgia
Atlanta

Slave auctions were common in Atlanta from the 1850's. During that period, Atlanta had a population that included 493 African slaves and 18 free men. As Atlanta became more prosperous, the number of slaves increased.

By 1870, the African American population in Atlanta represented 46 percent of the city's 21,700 residents. They competed for jobs and living space with whites who were poor migrants from the Georgia piedmont. The whites maintained a system of racial segregation to ensure white supremacy. For this reason, African Americans resided in their own communities, predominantly in east and west of downtown Atlanta. Most were common laborers, but a small number were businessmen, educators, clergy, and other professionals. A few African Americans made good income catering to whites in personal services such as barbering, dressmaking, and in building trades such as carpentry. Before desegregation, African Americans created their own opportunities in other areas such as publications and sports. Since the Atlanta public school system did not begin operations until 1872 and only three public grammar schools were opened to African Americans, the church and northern missionary societies opened private institutions such as Clark, Spelman, Morehouse, and Morris Brown colleges and Atlanta University. Atlanta was transformed into a regional center of higher education for African Americans.

Today, Atlanta is known for its concentration of an elite population of African Americans and Blacks who immigrated from other countries. One reason for their high achievements is that many graduates from the historically Black colleges and universities have remained in the city and have gained employment in influential positions. Another reason is that segregation laws after the 1906 Atlanta Race Riot caused the population to move to more secure locations where business owners could safely establish, expand, and provide services to their supportive communities. From that time until now, African Americans and others of African descent have continued to move to Atlanta which is known for its economic opportunities for people of color; consistent political leadership power; prosperous post-secondary institutions with high enrollment; dynamic arts, music, and sports cultures. The wealth of a large Black upper-class population is noticeable throughout the city. Atlanta is also recognized for its association with the civil rights movement, historic sites and monuments.

Morehouse College

Morehouse College is an historical Black college that was founded to provide post-secondary education in ministry and teaching to emancipated male students. The college opened in 1867 under the name Augusta Institute. It was supported by the American Baptist Home Mission Society through Springfield Baptist Church in Augusta, GA during Reconstruction. The founders were Rev. William Jefferson White, Rev. Edmund Turney, and former slave, Rev. Richard C. Coulter. The operations of the school were affected by financial problems, so it temporarily closed on a number of occasions. The New Georgia Encyclopedia (2006) includes information that the school also was impacted by the negativity of the white population to the institution's existence. The tensions became worse when the whites forced one of the school's leaders out of town on finding out he criticized their bad practices in a letter to the newspaper. In 1871, the school experienced a period of stability, but enrollment was still a challenge. The school relocated to the Friendship Baptist Church in Atlanta in 1879 and became known as Atlanta Baptist Seminary. The noise and smoke from the adjacent railroad yard and lumber mill presented challenges that impacted teaching classes and caused another move in 1885 to premises on 14 acres (The New Georgia Encyclopedia, 2006). The school became known as the Atlanta Baptist College in 1897 and offered its first baccalaureate degrees. Such changes steered the institution on the path of success since it acquired a reputation of educating leaders. In 1913 the final name change was made to Morehouse College. The Great Depression significantly affected the school's population growth and operations during the 1930s. However, by the 1940s the only HBCU for men regained its high status in the areas of scholarship and service. The progresses were evidenced by an increase of faculty with doctoral degrees, accreditation by the Southern Association of Colleges and Schools (SACS), and the establishment of the fraternity, Phi Beta Kappa chapter.

The school's accomplishments also included the ambitious task of opening a medical school in 1975; however, the medical institution was privatized in 1981. Morehouse College continued to prosper during the 1980s with an increase in the endowment to over $60 million which subsequently triggered a growth in faculty salary, student scholarships, and building expansions. The inauguration of the premier event, 'A Candle in the Dark Gala', occurred in 1989 and remains a popularly attended function every year since then. The 1990s saw the opening of the Andrew Young Center for International Affairs and the Morehouse Leadership Program. During the 21st century, Morehouse College has not only continued with its bold costly construction ventures and exceeding million-dollar campaign contribution goals, but it has also achieved academic success with graduates who have gone on to become Rhodes scholars. The school continues a steady path of success since the National Science Foundation ranked Morehouse as the top institution in graduating African-American men with doctorate degrees. The Atlanta University Center's (AUC) Robert W. Woodruff Library serves as custodian for the Morehouse College Martin Luther King Jr. Collection. The collection includes the famous "I Have a Dream" and the Nobel Peace Prize acceptance speeches (The New Georgia Encyclopedia, 2006).

Spelman College

Two white school teachers realized a need to educate emancipated women in Atlanta, Georgia. They collaborated with the pastor at Friendship Baptist Church and sought the assistance of the Women's American Baptist Home Mission Society, a New England organization that provided funding to open and maintain the Atlanta Female Baptist Seminary in 1881 (The New Georgia Encyclopedia, 2006). The historically Black, liberal arts college for women began with ten students including former slaves. The desire for knowledge was evident as enrollment of women quickly increased to 100 students who were not deterred in taking classes in the church's basement. However, the over-crowded atmosphere meant that it was time for the school to move to a more suitable location. Classes were taught by four white women from the north, two of whom developed a connection with the oil magnate John D. Rockefeller and his wife Laura Spelman Rockefeller at a church conference in 1882. Through this pivotal connection, the wealthy couple made a generous donation to the school that enabled its relocation to a nine-acre property (Common Fund, 2009). Two years later when the Rockefellers were invited to the college's third-year anniversary celebration of the seminary, they were shown gratitude for their generosity with the renaming of the school to Spelman Seminary in honor of Mrs. Rockefeller's family. A board of directors and charter were established in 1888 (The New Georgia Encyclopedia, 2006).

The influence of the Rockefellers with the college meant that for decades the school was run by white presidents from the northeast who were friends of the wealthy family. They introduced their strict standards of decorum expected from women in the Victorian era which included wearing hats and gloves in public. The students also needed written permission when travelling off campus. They were expected to participate in domestic training classes to learn sewing, cooking, and laundry work. Students were even required to wake up as early as 4:30 A.M. every morning to wash and iron their clothes. This practice was implemented by the founders who believed former slaves possessed undisciplined work habits. The insensitive action against the students persisted for approximately 40 years after the school's inception.

While Spelman College was opened during the late 1900s, public high schools were non-existent for former slaves and their descendants throughout Georgia. As a result, the Spelman ladies initially had to enroll in high school equivalency courses prior to undertaking post-secondary courses. The college awarded diplomas to the first high school graduates in 1887. Post-secondary courses focused primarily on teacher training to meet the high demand for teachers after emancipation. Students received practical experience during the summer months by teaching not only throughout the Georgia countryside but also the rural communities of other southern states. By 1886, the school began to focus on the need for nurses by providing a nursing program. A missionary training program was initiated in 1891. The first baccalaureate degrees were awarded in 1901. In 1924, the name was officially changed to Spelman College.

Spelman College students participated with their peers from other colleges in sit-ins at businesses in downtown Atlanta during the 1960s Civil Rights protests. The young ladies maintained that tradition of activism in 2004 by protesting a musician's impending visit to the campus. That performer's activism in promoting bone marrow donation was not enough for him to be welcomed on campus because he was known for his disrespectful, misogynistic videos. The outcry of Spelman College students triggered the performer's cancellation of his appearance on campus.

The college has consistently maintained high enrollment throughout the years, and as of 2005, approximately 2, 300 students were in attendance with a staff of 150 full-time faculty. The college expanded its offerings to 26 majors and 25 minors. A benefit for the institution is its signing in 1929 of an "Agreement of Affiliation" in which students at Spelman College may also register to take classes at other partnering institutions such as Morehouse College and Clark Atlanta University. Spelman College has also maintained financial stability, unlike other historically Black colleges, since it acquired $300 million, which has been considered the largest endowment of any historically Black college or university in the United States.

Florida
Tallahassee

Leon County, which includes the city of Tallahassee, led the state of Florida in cotton production. The county also had the greatest cluster of plantations in the state. Tallahassee became the center of Florida's slave trade. Prior to the official abolition of slavery, Leon County's slaves totaled 73 percent of the population in 1860, and almost all of them were slaves (Rivers, 1981). In fact, Leon County was the dwelling of more slaves than in any other county in Florida. The Florida State Capitol building is presumed to have been constructed by slaves from this large, free labor force. When President Abraham Lincoln issued the Emancipation Proclamation in 1863, many believed that slavery ended. However, freedom did not immediately occur for slaves in Florida. Tallahassee was the first town in Florida to hear the official ending of slavery in that state with a reading of the Emancipation Proclamation at the state's Capitol building on May 20, 1865.

After the Civil War, many of the emancipated slaves established their own communities because African Americans were prohibited from purchasing land and residing in white communities. In addition, segregation was evident in schools, churches, stores, movie theaters, hospitals, parks, cemeteries, and on the public busses. A hook and ladder company was necessary for the African American community because the white-manned fire station in the city would only respond to fires in their own neighborhoods. Residents were instrumental in the fight for desegregation with a bus boycott, a series of sit-ins at the lunch counter of Woolworth, and other demonstrations. The whites' cruel tactics made African Americans in Tallahassee live in fear of lynching. Tallahassee became known for the highest lynching per capita in Florida from

1900 to 1930. Blacks had to deal with blatant racial injustices and segregation tactics from the end of Reconstruction until the early 1970s

The 2010 census indicated that the African American population in Tallahassee decreased to 34 percent. Nevertheless, the community continues to recognize their culture by organizing events such as Juneteenth, the commemoration of the Emancipation Proclamation. The event is celebrated on May 20th of each year at the Knott House where the proclamation was read on May 20, 1865. Other Black cultural places of interest in Tallahassee include the John G. Riley Center/Museum of African American History & Culture and the Carrie Meek and James N. Eaton, Sr., Southeastern Regional Black Archives Research Center and Museum. The city has progressed from being known as the most racist city in Florida to one now regarded as tolerant with a diverse population.

Florida Agriculture & Mechanic University (FAMU)

The passage of the Second Morrill Act in 1890 required states with segregated whites-only higher education institutions to expand their public land-grant system to include institutions where the students of African descent could enroll (Finkelman, 2009). The act opened the door for schools such as Florida Agriculture & Mechanic University to be designated as a land-grant college in Tallahassee. State Normal College for Colored Students, as it was initially known, was established in 1887 in Florida's capital city, Tallahassee. Fifteen students were taught by two instructors in a single building. After the college was awarded $7,500 in land-grant funds and also property, it was relocated to a better site and its present location. During the 1890s the institution became known as the State Normal and Industrial College for Colored Students.

Trustees saw the land-grant award as an advantage in promoting the school's vocational education program.

Finkelman (2009) reports that during the 1900s the college prospered as a school where agricultural education was promoted for African-American farmhands. But, President Young, having a liberal arts background, wanted to also introduce liberal arts and industrial education into the curriculum. He was aware that the white community would object to African American students learning anything else but agriculture, so he assured them that he would continue the status quo. Instead, President Young worked diligently in a confidential venture with trustworthy personnel to establish programs in the arts and sciences along with raising the university programs to the level of accreditation. The trustees did not appreciate learning that the college became a four-year degree granting institution that offered B.Sc. degrees in education, science, home economics, agriculture and mechanical arts. So, they attempted to force President Young to concentrate entirely on the industrial programs. However, progress could not be deterred, when the Board of Control took over management of the college from the Board of Education. The college was designated as an institution of higher learning and became known as Florida Agricultural and Mechanical College for Negroes (FAMC). Enrollment continued to increase, and the first degrees were awarded in 1910. President Young withstood the confrontations of those who did not want the school to progress, and he aired his dissatisfactions on the restrictions that were placed to impact education for African Americans. His departure from the school allowed the board to select a president with similar preferences that caused the school to re-focus on vocational education with an emphasis on farming. The departure from offering liberal education classes angered students and alumnae who protested and boycotted classes. Several buildings on campus were mysteriously burned down. Leadership of the college was eventually assumed by President Lee who stressed academic excellence similar to President Young. His tenure is remembered for the expansions on campus, additional land purchases, and an increase in faculty. During President Lee's tenure, white politicians turned down an offer from Andrew Carnegie to build a library in the city of Tallahassee because they resisted the clause that the library had to serve all including African-American residents. But, after negotiations with the FAMC, a Carnegie grant of $10,000 was awarded for the construction of a new library on the school's campus to replace the one previously destroyed by a fire.

During the early 1920s FAMC introduced Bachelor of Science degrees in education, science, home economics, agriculture, and mechanical arts. Student enrollment continued to grow from 1949 to 1953 when the institution's status was changed to a university. The upgrade brought an expansion of graduate level programs and building construction. The name changed to Florida Agricultural and Mechanical University (FAMU) without the racial connotation presented in previous names. The Supreme Court decision in 1954 to desegregate all schools was beneficial to FAMU because more funding was available. Furthermore, the school's expansions began to take on an indifferent outlook for white residents whose priority focused on surviving during the Depression and World War II instead of concentrating on fears that educated African Americans could disrupt the country (Finkelman, 2009).

Students from FAMU were whole-heartedly involved in protesting the injustices that African Americans experienced in Tallahassee during the 1960s. In fact, two female students refused to give up their seats on a bus in Tallahassee and were arrested by police in 1956 prior to the experiences and prominence given to Rosa Parks who took a similar action. The arrest triggered FAMU students, the local NAAACP chapter, and ministers to join forces to boycott the Tallahassee public transportation system. Finkelman (2009) outlines that in spite of the Florida State Legislature's threatening policies to end protests, students secretly continued the efforts. Protestors also took to the streets to voice support for an Afro-American student who was raped by four white men who, quite surprisingly, were convicted. Students got involved in the Civil Rights movement by boycotting public facilities, taking on the need to desegregated stores, and increasing voter registration. Such activism demonstrated that students, as educated persons, could influence society. During these turbulent periods, FAMU continued its expansions, and by 1971 the institution became recognized as one of the nine universities forming a partnership in the public higher-education system of Florida. This recognition increased the school's ranking to an all-time high in enrolling National Achievement finalists which surpassed some Ivy League institutions.

The school has been engulfed in controversies during the 21st century. There have been administrative scandals, investigations on mismanagement of funds, and penalization from the National Collegiate Athletic Association (NCAA). But, the hazing death of a member of the university's infamous marching band, suspension of the band, plus arrest and conviction of its members attacked increased public scrutiny. Despite that issue, the opening of a law school and other new programs have caused significant enrollment increases of students which include those from various states and all over the world.

Tennessee
Nashville

Nashville was an overwhelmingly pro-slavery city with a thriving slave trade. In the1860 U.S. slave census, approximately 14,600 slaves and 1,209 freemen with restricted rights lived in Nashville. In addition to slave owners, the government of Nashville owned slaves. This problem was evident when two out of the government's 26 slaves escaped. Even more repulsive was that the mayor of Nashville purchased runaway slave ads to track them down. In the 1840s and 1850s, a series of slave trading businesses were prevalent throughout Nashville. The businesses held regular slave trades and 150 to 200 captives including young children were kept in slave pens where people could see those who were on sale (Carey, 2018). From the pen, hundreds were routinely taken and sold at the Davidson County Courthouse. In addition, others were sold at Nashville's Public Square Park where people met to shop, mingle, conduct business, and celebrate events. This was a horrifying experience for slaves who were devalued and separated by their public sale. The chancery court clerk and master carried out many of the sales. Carey (2018) mentions that slave labor was used to construct the Tennessee State Capitol. The involvement of slaves in the construction is supported by a report in the Republican Banner which contains news that a sad accident caused the death of a slave while working on the building in 1848.

Reports indicate a decline in the African-American population in Nashville. Gentrification is one cause since some communities have been impacted by new property developments that have increased the cost of living and created the possible elimination of long-standing African American neighborhoods (George, n.d.). However, some of the city's cultural staples, residents, and African-American owned businesses remain in other Black communities to preserve the traditions of the neighborhood. Furthermore, African Americans are still the second largest demographic in the city. In the last few years, the city has seen growth in their business and cultural endeavors. In addition, Forbes magazine analyst and contributor, Pete Saunders, notes that Black incomes in Nashville have been rising most rapidly since 2010 (Kotkin and Cox, 2018).

Meharry Medical College and the School of Medicine

Prior to and after emancipation throughout the south, many hospitals and doctors refused to provide care to freed persons who needed medical attention. A Methodist clergymen and laymen from the Freedmen's Aid Society in Nashville, Tennessee, recognized a need to open a medical department at Central Tennessee College, an institution founded for freedmen in 1865. The venture was expected to produce medical personnel who would attend to the care of African Americans denied necessary health services. Samuel Meharry heard about the project and pledged to support the establishment of the medical department. The promise was made approximately 40 years after Samuel Meharry's encounter with former slaves who assisted him at the age of 16 years old when his wagon, filled with salt, got stuck in a muddy ditch. His gratitude to the slaves was never forgotten. He made all effort to follow through with his pledge to repay their act of kindness by collaborating with his brothers to give a substantial donation to building the medical school in honor of the slaves. The donation funded the work and opening of Meharry Medical Department at Central Tennessee College in 1876. The institution was the first medical training department in the south for former slaves who far too long had been denied an opportunity to train in the health sector because of their race. The first director of the department was Dr. George

W. Hubbard. The department admitted its first 11 students who were instructed by two faculty members in the basement of Clark Memorial United Methodist Church. Admission was initially based on students either possessing a high school diploma or passing an entrance exam until 1914 when students had to first enroll in pre-medical education courses (Lovett, 1999). The department quickly distinguished itself as a medical school by adding nursing and dental programs within 10 years. The pharmacy program opened in 1889. In 1900 Central Tennessee College became Walden University and the medical department was renamed Meharry Medical College of Walden. The Flexner Report, which provided a critique of medical schools, rated Meharry as "the most creditable institution" and that "the upbuilding of…Meharry will profit the nation". The high rating provided the medical college with financial backing to continue enrollment and use desperately needed funding to renovate buildings thereby improving the quality of medical training for its students. Meharry Medical College of Walden became the first medical school in the south to offer four years of training. In 1915, the medical department was renamed Meharry Medical College and became an independent institution after receiving a new state charter.

During the initial operations of the medical college, it struggled to gain the respect and confidence from its own freedmen community. Budget problems prevented the maintenance of a first-rate hospital and doctors lacked enough clinical laboratory experiences to perform complicated medical procedures. Their own community believed that students were stealing bodies to perform lab work (Lovett, 1999). Furthermore, the medical students did not have the privilege of training at City Hospital. Dr. Robert Boyd, a prominent Meharry graduate, realizing the dire need for clinical experience, opened the 23-bed private

Mercy Hospital to provide Meharry medical students with the opportunity to obtain clinical training (Hansen, 1962). However, years later due to disagreements among doctors within the hospital, Dr. Boyd suggested the need for the medical school to start their own clinical teaching facility. The George W. Hubbard Hospital Association formed, with Dr. Boyd as chairman, to raise funds to erect a hospital to serve as a training facility for medical students. The Hubbard Hospital's first partially completed unit was opened in 1910 as a clinical teaching facility for the medical college. By 1912, the fully completed two-story building was officially dedicated and began accepting as many as 80 patients (Hansen, 1962). Initially, the facilities were quite limited, so the hospital's stability was affected by closures and re-openings. Endowment from the Rockefeller Foundation and other foundations enabled the hospital to begin expansion to serve the needs of so many patients who could not afford to pay for their medical needs.

The hospital has gone through not only a series of major renovations, but there also have been name changes throughout the years. It operated under the name Metro General Hospital and is currently known as Nashville General Hospital when the government of Nashville and Davidson County moved its public hospital to Meharry's campus in 1994. Nashville General Hospital at Meharry continues to be the principle teaching hospital for Meharry's clinical training. The hospital has a unique and controversial public versus private collaboration involving Meharry Medical College, Vanderbilt University Medical Center, and the Metropolitan Nashville Hospital Authority. In spite of the difficulties it faces from time to time, Meharry Medical College and the hospital continue to unite to provide care at the city's only public hospital.

The British Caribbean Journey

British Colonies and Education

The British Caribbean includes countries that were colonized by England and served as a destination for the transportation of African slaves. There, they were sold and subjected to cruelty while they labored on plantations and in the houses of British colonists. Those countries include Anguilla, Antigua & Barbuda, The Bahamas, Barbados, Belize, Bermuda, British Virgin Islands, Cayman Islands, Dominica, Grenada, Guyana, Jamaica, Montserrat, St. Kitts & Nevis, St. Lucia, St. Vincent & the Grenadines, Trinidad & Tobago, and Turks & Caicos Islands. The British slave trade officially ended in 1807, but slavery continued until emancipation, August 1st, 1834. The British dominated the slave trade and transported an estimate of 2.7 million slaves to the western world.

After emancipation, British colonists were convinced by the English government that it was in their best interest to maintain control of former slaves by providing primary/elementary school education only. The yearning of former slaves for education resulted in steady increase of their enrollment in primary school. By 1841 in Guyana, 101 primary schools were opened for a significant number of children (Ishmael, 2014). By 1862, 232 new government-run primary schools were opened throughout Jamaica (King, 1998).

In contrast to the massive expansion of the primary schools, there was a demand for secondary education especially for those children of African descent who were thought to be exceptionally talented and deserved more than to attend a basic primary school However, many legislators were unwilling to increase the funds for education, especially secondary education for Afro-Caribbean children who they believed were destined to work in agriculture. The estate owners wanted to continue securing persons who would form the pool of workers for which their estate labor forces could be chosen. Former slaves were ambitious and knew that upward mobility could be achieved through continuing education. Some elementary schools also encouraged their students by informing them of the opportunities of continuing to learn beyond basic education. British colonists were threatened by the desires of Afro-Caribbean persons to raise their status in society through education. So, many strategies were in place to prevent former African slaves and biracial children from attending secondary schools that could have made them progress in society. The fee structure of secondary schools was increased so Afro-Caribbean parents could not afford the costs. According to Bacchus (1996), in Trinidad, even some government secondary schools charged excessive fees that were beyond the financial capability of most parents, especially those at the lower levels of the social and economic hierarchy. Another strategy was using social exclusiveness of the secondary schools to refuse all illegitimate children the ability to enroll. For instance, the principal of the Lodge School argued a case for denying illegitimate children, regardless of their learning achievements, from gaining acceptance into the most prestigious secondary schools in Barbados. In Jamaica the Wesleyans were criticized for expelling two illegitimate children at York Castle High School. Even, Wolmer's School took a different route some years after emancipation and reduced their enrollment to non-white students. (Bacchus, 1996). Eventually, the legislature of Barbados voted to provide scholarships to a selected few gifted Afro-Barbadian students from marital households. Providing a limited number of scholarships gave a false impression that students could achieve occupational and social progress in spite of their color or race. In reality, the British colonists did not intend to radically change the existing race and class stratification since grammar schools continued to recruit predominantly from the elite class in the society. So, during the late 1900s children from middle class and elite families enjoyed benefits of state-subsidized education that would have been more deserved by needy students. In addition, instructions in the primary schools attended by Afro-Caribbean students were below standards, so students faced difficulties in passing the entrance examination to the secondary schools. In one instance in Trinidad, only nine students received scholarships out of the 24 awards that were available for non-white students (Bacchus, 1996).

Jamaica
Education During and After Slavery

Before the Emancipation Act in 1834, Jamaica had no formal education system for slaves, ex-slaves, biracial and indigenous people. However, some had the opportunity of attending plantation schools established for boys by foreign missionaries, and a few plantations schools accepted girls. The curriculum for those children was based on religion and the virtues of submission (King, 1998). An established education system was also not in place either for whites, so the wealthy sent their children instead to England or hired private tutors if they could afford to do so. Others who were less affluent sent their children to one of the free schools that were established from the bequest of wealthy planters or merchants. These free schools for those children included Wolmer's, Mannings, Beckford and Smith (now known as St. Jago), Russea's, Tichfield, York Castle, and Jamaica College. The curriculum of such schools was based on similar courses and standards provided to students who attended schools in England.

Following emancipation, the missionaries responded to the lack of organized education for ex-slaves and other free people of color by establishing a structured elementary education system. The British eventually surmised that it would be in their best interest to establish their own education system to integrate ex-slaves into building England's economy and to also ensure that a lower class of peaceful people remained intact and reliant on the mother land. This system was not undertaken by the British government until shortly after the 1865 Morant Bay Rebellion that uncovered great dissention of Jamaicans with the British system of government. The British education system provided students with classes in reading, writing, and arithmetic along with some religious education, but the main focus was agricultural training for boys so that they would eventually gain employment on the estates where they would grow crops for export that would be a financial benefit to England. Agricultural training was also emphasized to stop the economic threat to England as dissatisfied rural dwellers began to migrate from the countryside to the cities and towns. Education for girls, on the other hand, included sewing and domestic science to provide them with skills to work in white family households. These educational practices continued throughout the early 20th century, a period when education remained uncommon for most Jamaicans especially beyond the primary level.

The elitist curriculum promoted class divisions in colonial society that included a dual system of education which barred a large part of the population from attaining more than functional literacy. The poor majority were expected to attend and end their schooling at the elementary school level while the privileged and powerful minority groups were expected to gain additional schooling by attending and completing secondary school. In the late 1800s, some secondary schools in Kingston served primarily the light-skinned elite (Global Foundation to Upgrade Underserved Primary and Secondary School, n.d.). The government's Board of Education was responsible for the administration of the policies for the elementary school system while the day-to-day operations were conducted by school managers who were appointed from different religious denominations that owned the majority of the schools. The head teacher, usually a religious minister, reported the school business to his manager. On the other hand, school commissions had independent authority to run secondary institutions. They reported to a school board managed by a Board of Governors that could hire and fire teachers, administer financial affairs, set salaries for teachers, set school policy with respect to student admissions and other matters. The two separate educational systems were in place for over 70 years. Teachers' colleges were combined into the elementary school systems but came under the jurisdiction of the board. Fee-paying private preparatory schools offering primary education were integrated into the secondary school system and came under the jurisdiction of the schools' commission. In 1943, fewer than one percent of Afro-Jamaicans and only nine percent of the biracial population attended secondary school. (Meditz and Hanratty, 1987).

Due to an increase in funding for education in 1944, a national education policy was developed that advanced the possibilities of education for all and redefined educational priorities. Meditz and Hanratty (1987) wrote that through the establishment of the Ministry of Education in 1953 and independence in 1962, the government constructed additional primary schools and fifty junior secondary schools (grades seven, eight, and nine). But, up until the 1970s, the educational system continued to provide insufficient opportunities at the post-primary levels, so many of the inherited problems from the British educational system remained.

The major reform of secondary education during the populist era was the creation of five different types of Jamaican secondary schools. These secondary schools were established during the 1940s with the conversion and re-naming of 16 senior schools to junior secondary schools and the building of 50 new schools (Miller, 1990). The establishment of 66 junior secondary schools constituted the largest single investment in education in the post-independence period. These were three-year schools, with non-selective, free flow, feeder school entry and a broad-based curriculum. Almost immediately after the creation of these three-year schools, they were converted into five-year institutions and renamed new secondary schools during the 1970s. Their enrollment by 1978 was approximately 80,000 students, which was more than all the other types of secondary schools combined (Miller, 1990). The new secondary school was different from the other types of secondary schools because: it followed the community concept, its curriculum was geared towards vocational training, and it did not require students to take England's Cambridge examinations. Of course, these expectations placed them in a category lower than the traditional secondary schools, so the new secondary schools attracted low achieving students from disadvantaged backgrounds although it offered the greatest access to secondary education. The new secondary schools also did not live up to the reform anticipations of UNESCO and the World Bank to increase equality in the Jamaican educational system. The traditional high schools continued to represent elitist education that catered largely to the middle and upper classes, so their selective enrollment increased the social divisions. But, ironically, the lower social classes placed the highest importance on gaining acceptance into these elite schools. People's perceptions were that the foreign aid organizations should have concentrated their secondary school expansion efforts on the elite schools thereby opening up more opportunities for others to enroll in them. But, on the other hand, those who benefited most from traditional secondary school education were not eager for any expansions that would crowd their schools with the majority of the population. Those elitist views reflect the new secondary school as the best option to maintain a division among the population. Research confirms that the new secondary reforms have contributed to further strengthening the historical divisions among secondary schools instead of reducing social inequities that these schools should have generated into the society. Miller

(1990), in a tracer study of secondary school leavers transitioning to youth labor, reports that the market was segmented because traditional secondary schools and new secondary schools supplied different levels of workers. In 1998, the new secondary schools were upgraded to comprehensive high schools. They achieved high school status in 2000.

Another type of secondary school is the technical high school. They were established because of a need to restructure trade training centers into high schools with a technical emphasis. These schools were expected to be accessible to those students who did not qualify to attend the traditional secondary schools but had the potential to excel in technical or vocational subjects. Technical schools were funded by a grant from the Carnegie Foundation during the early 1940s. However, the growth of this educational concept was slow since there were only six technical schools by 1978 (Miller, 1990).

The comprehensive high school was another new form of secondary education introduced to the Jamaican school system during the 1960s. The concept of opening comprehensive high schools in different communities was not only for them to become feeder schools to the surrounding primary schools but also to combine the academic and technical skills needed for the workplace. The model was initially implemented in two schools but never gained popularity. The comprehensive designation was removed, and they are now known as high or secondary schools

Vocational high schools were another experiment in secondary education policy. Two schools were created in rural communities to get students interested and involved in the technical and practical aspects of agriculture that would lead them to agricultural careers. The programs lasted for two to three years and accepted students who completed Grade 9.

During the late 1950s, the government introduced the Common Entrance exam to establish a system that would provide all Jamaican students with an opportunity to vie for placement into a secondary school. However, the Common Entrance and its subsequent replacement exams have segregated students based on their learning abilities. Students with top scores, more often than not, will attend the traditional secondary schools while those with lower scores are placed instead in the new secondary schools. As a result, the unbalanced secondary school placement trend has caused the traditional secondary schools to continuously produce students who outperform those attending the new secondary schools.

Kingston Parish

Kingston was founded in 1692 when most of the 4,000 survivors moved inland to that area after an earthquake and tsunami destroyed their residences in Port Royal, the former major town. Kingston became the largest town in Jamaica by 1716 and its deep-water harbor made it the center of trade for the entire British colony. By 1778 Kingston had a population of 26,478, which included 16,659 enslaved people (Black Past, n.d.). However, the 1811 Jamaican Almanac indicates a decrease in the slave population in Kingston since it shows approximately 13,000 slaves although an official count could only be given for the 6,500 slaves whose owners paid taxes. After emancipation, many freed persons living throughout rural communities migrated to Kingston in search of a better life. This took them away not only from the drudgery of cultivating land on former plantations but also from discriminatory practices. However, they encountered even more prejudices since employers preferred to hire biracial Jamaicans or those with a lighter shade black skin tone. Kingston became the official capital of the colony of Jamaica in 1872. The city was destroyed in 1907 by an earthquake. Over 1,000 residents perished, many of whom died when their homes were engulfed in flames because of the earthquake.

Wolmer's Boys School and Immaculate Conception High School, located in downtown Kingston, were destroyed by the earthquake. Both schools were relocated to other premises away from the downtown area. The building occupied by Kingston Technical High School was also destroyed. However, it was rebuilt on the same downtown Hanover Street landmark site that the school has occupied since 1896. Other landmarks on that same premises are the B block building which was the headmaster's quarters during the early 1900s. The masonic temple is another national heritage building that is located on the premises.

Deteriorating residential and commercial buildings that once represented the grandeur and opulence of colonial life for the white ruling class still exist throughout downtown Kingston. One prominent building depicting colonial rule is the Kingston Tower Street Adult Correctional Centre, previously known as General Penitentiary. The massive building was constructed by former slaves during the 1840s to incarcerate approximately 600 Jamaicans like themselves who were former slaves. This is one of the few structures built during the colonial era in downtown Kingston that is still used for the purpose it was intended in spite of its current over-crowded, unsanitary conditions.

Kingston College

Kingston College was an anomaly in the Jamaican education system during an era when poor Jamaican children were not readily accepted into secondary schools. Bishop DeCarteret was aware of a plethora of untapped brilliance among children from poor and lower middle-class families living throughout the capital city of Kingston and also St. Andrews. So, he defied the unjust practices of the colonial school system by founding Kingston College which opened its doors on April 16, 1925 in the city of Kingston to any male child who wanted to obtain a secondary education regardless of their skin color, their parents' marital status, incapacity to satisfy the entrance requirements, or inability to afford the costs to attend a secondary school. Under the leadership of Bishop Percival Gibson as the first headmaster, 49 Jamaican boys entered the school on the first day of its inception. The school initially opened on an East Street property purchased by Bishop Gibson and his sister from the former All Saints Rectory. These boys had an opportunity to overcome the social injustices that confined poor children of African descent to primary school education only. They were among the first set of students whose academic and athletic abilities were nurtured at Kingston College. The opening of Kingston College signified the courageous efforts that had been finally implemented to emancipate the colonial education system. By 1932, the school became a government grant-aided secondary school which alleviated it from the financial needs of maintaining its operations. The school was relocated from this initial site in 1934 to the North Street premises when land was purchased from the Boy Scouts Association. By 1948, Kingston College became the largest secondary school with an enrollment of 500 boys. The student population growth caused a need for additional space. So, land was purchased from the Melbourne Cricket Club to accommodate the increase.

Today, the two campuses remain with upper level students attending the North Street campus while beginning and lower level students are taught at the Melbourne campus. The school is noted for academic programs and strong sports traditions, but it is also recognized for a world class boys' choir, the Kingston College Chapel Choir, that not only gives concerts locally but overseas. The Kingston College Development Trust Fund was established in 1986. Its committee serves to raise funds to assist with the renovations, new constructions, and intended work to modernize the facilities on both campuses. The alumnae association also plays an important part in giving back to the school by funding projects so that students will continue to receive top education.

Kingston Technical High School

Kingston Technical High School is considered the first technical high school in the English-speaking Caribbean. It was opened at a time when approximately 3,000 school spaces were needed to accommodate children especially those in Kingston (The Daily Gleaner, 1911). The Board of Education addressed the problem by establishing a large elementary school with three divisions which included a kindergarten and also a department for boys and another department for girls with separate gender-based curriculum. During the colonial period, a bias persisted among the ruling white class against providing economically disadvantaged Jamaican children with secondary education, so implementing manual training courses was perhaps the best option for the board to insinuate that they were addressing the secondary education needs of the majority population. Of course, a great desire to be educated made attending manual training school an acceptable continuing alternative that would enable Jamaicans to learn a trade at a government school. Known as the Board School, it was opened in 1896 on Hanover Street on premises formerly occupied by Mico Normal School (The Daily Gleaner, 1911). The name was changed shortly thereafter to Manual Training School. Children from Kingston were the first to gain entry and receive technical instructions. By 1901, the girls' department closed, but the boys' department remained open to provide manual training courses (A. Sangster, 2011). The elementary school stayed open also to serve primarily as a training facility where aspiring teachers would gain practical teaching experience. By 1907, after the earthquake, the government needed to use the partially destroyed Hanover Street premises. So, the elementary school was temporarily closed, but the manual training school was relocated to Elletson Road. By 1913, all departments re-occupied the premises on Hanover Street. The manual school continued to offer classes in woodwork, metalwork, and home economic. New courses included structural engineering, machine shop practice, welding, electrical installation, commercial subjects and handicrafts. In 1918 the school extended its continuing education training to World War I disabled soldiers who were given instruction in tailoring, shoe-making, carpentry, and metalwork. The growth in office jobs during the 1950s through the 1960s created a need to introduce courses in shorthand and typing. Prior to settling with the name Kingston Technical High School or KTHS, the institution went through other name changes such as Government Technical and Continuation School; Technical and Commercial School; and Government, Technical, and Continuation School.

Kingston Technical High School served as a model in opening other technical schools throughout the island. The school changed its admissions policies by starting to enroll students from the grade 9 level, but since 2008, students have begun enrolling from the grade 7 level. Throughout the years, the school also added academic subjects to its curriculum. This addition provides students with more opportunities because some may now focus on completing an academic track that is similar to the curriculum at a traditional secondary school. Students may also consider incorporating both academics with technical courses.

St. Andrews Parish

Slaves not only resided in Kingston but in the adjacent upper hillside and lower plains of St. Andrews. The area was previously known as Liguanea, and it was formerly changed to St. Andrews when the town was established by law in 1867. The 1833 Jamaica Almanac includes records of 5,265 slaves on the sugar plantations of Constant Spring, Norbrook, Shortwood, and Temple Hall. Others could be found on Mona, Papine, and Hope sugar estates. After the decline of sugar, these estates were turned into experimental plantations where slaves planted and reaped different types of crops. Ruins dating back to the Mona Estate period can still be found on that property. These include the water wheel, mills, and aqueducts built and worked by slaves. In addition, the University of the West Indies' Mona Campus is housed on both the former Mona and Papine sugar plantations. Shortwood Teacher's College is located on the former Shortwood Estate. In the 2011 census, a population of 573,369 resided in St. Andrew. This was the highest number of residents in any of the parishes in Jamaica.

August is a special month in Jamaica when the country celebrates Emancipation Day on August 1st and Independence Day on the first Mondays of August. One of the popular cultural activities that is entrenched in the customs of Jamaicans during that month is the Grand Gala celebrations that takes place annually in St. Andrews at the Jamaica National Stadium. This gala connects people with their history through music, dance, and drama performances depicting life during former eras. The celebration also includes the coming together of a selected number of children throughout the island for impressive routines. This culminates months of competitions in the arts where top performers receive prizes. In addition, the Grand Gala showcases the winner of the national song contest, well-known performers, and personalities. The gala not only takes Jamaicans back in time but also recognizes how culture has changed throughout the years to the present.

Shortwood Teachers College

After the abolition of slavery in 1834, a great need existed for teachers to educate the masses of emancipated slaves. When Mico Normal School was established in 1835 shortly after the abolition of slavery, the primary goal was to train British volunteers from England and those expatriates residing on the island to teach children of ex-slaves. After the steady growth of primary schools throughout the island, Shortwood Normal School was not only opened as a female teachers' training counterpart to Mico's male teachers' training college, but it was established to address a need to train Jamaican female teachers who could better relate to the racial and cultural learning development of children throughout the island. However, efforts did not begin to materialize until 1880 after its approval was included in a package for social, economic, and political reforms. The overwhelming support from educators and government officials were also instrumental in the opening of the Jamaica Female Training College in 1885 with an enrollment of 18 students. The enrollment number appeared to be minimal in comparison to so many children on the island who would have been attending elementary school. Nevertheless, the college provided necessary teaching skills to outstanding students who could not afford to attend a secondary school and those who completed secondary school but could not afford to go to a university in England.

The government financed college initially occupied premises in Barbican, St. Andrews. But, due to an outbreak of yellow fever in the Barbican area in 1885, the school was relocated to Camperdown, St. Andrews. After purchase of the Shortwood Estate in St. Andrews, the college was relocated in 1887 to that premises where it remains today.

By 1889, the school's financial difficulties and impending closure were alleviated with an increase in student enrollment based on recommendations in the Lamb Report. Also, the addition of practical courses in varied areas such as agricultural science, gardening, laundry, and culinary arts was implemented to increase enrollment. Enrollment increased to 60 students. However, newly arriving students were expected to pay an annual tuition and boarding fees while those few earlier enrolled students were granted an exemption to continue with their free education. Of course, many students from low income households were financially unable to attend the college. Fees were discontinued in 1957. The return of free education at the college led to an increase in the student population. The student growth during the 1960s instigated construction of hostels and additional classrooms.

During the 1960s the new junior secondary schools were established to address the large increase of students who now were of the age to attend secondary schools but were not successful in passing the islands' high school entrance exam, the Common Entrance Exam. A large enrollment in new junior secondary schools during the 1960s ushered an innovative method of teacher training courses at the college where students were trained to teach in the secondary and post-secondary schools. The steep increase of the student population at the teachers' college also required expansion of faculty and residential campus housing.

In 1996, the college collaborated with the University of the West Indies to offer Bachelor of Education degree programs. In 2000, the college made further strides in its association by linking with the University of South Florida to provide a Master of Arts Degree in Early Childhood Education. During the early 2000, the primary education program was phased out and concentration was placed instead on secondary and early childhood education. The year 2001 was historic for the college when it became a co-educational institution and began accepting male students for the first time in its history. The institution continues to collaborate with universities, the private sector, the alumni association, and international organization to expand its offerings in the field of education.

Community Colleges and Excelsior Community College

Community colleges have changed the post-secondary education environment throughout Jamaica since their inception during the 1970s. Those colleges, especially in the rural areas, were initially established to provide sixth form or grade 12 program options for students especially those from secondary schools where sixth form enrollment had begun to decline over the years. In addition, community colleges became educational outlets for those who had to re-take subjects on the previously administered General Certificate Education (GCE) assessment and the current Caribbean Examinations Council (CXC) assessment. Years later, the community college system has transformed into an affordable and accessible option for so many who would not have had a chance to attend college. The population has grown rapidly throughout the years with an increase in enrollment of approximately 10,000 to 12,000. Students may enroll in a variety of programs that include continuing education, short courses, postgraduate diplomas, associate and bachelor's degree. This community college concept has been extended to Anguilla and the Turks and Caicos Island along with at the Bahamas Baptist Community College.

Excelsior Community College began as a pilot project in 1971 to serve as a teacher training center for full-time students who wanted to teach in the secondary school system. This pilot program expanded in 1972 when an evening division was opened to attract part-time students. The formal launching of the college occurred in 1974. During that time, courses were taught in the areas of teacher training, nursing education, business education to include secretarial studies, and pre-university education for incoming sixth form students, especially those from Excelsior High School.

University of the West Indies
Mona Campus

The difficulty for those Jamaican parents who could not afford to send their children to a tertiary institution abroad was addressed with the opening of the University College of the West Indies (UWI) Mona Campus in St. Andrews in 1948. Prior to the establishment of UWI, wealthy parents sent their children to universities in England or elsewhere abroad. During the colonial era, there were discussions of setting up a West Indian university with one of its main functions to write examinations especially for secondary schools in the West Indies. This idea did not receive enough support until the middle of the 20th century when an initiative for starting the University College of the West Indies came from the British government thereby resulting in its opening in 1948. Sir Philip Sherlock, referenced in a 1983 digital report, believes that the delay in establishing a local university stemmed from the colonial mentality that objected to uplifting the majority population in society and education. Therefore, Jamaican intellectuals who wanted to limit higher education to elites like themselves questioned the need to establish a local university.

The opening of the university enabled post-secondary education of home-grown talent that would give them opportunities for employment in senior positions that otherwise would be offered to expatriates recruited from England. But even more notable was that UWI welcomed students not only from Jamaica but from other Caribbean islands. During its first years, 33 students coming from Jamaica and throughout the Caribbean were enrolled in its medical program.

While the university provided an opportunity for Jamaicans and others to afford to obtain post-secondary education, its highly selective enrollment requirements made post-secondary education still unattainable by the majority population. So, UWI only partially addressed the problems that caused many high school leavers to seek post-secondary education abroad. However, in 2009, in response to a growing popularity of virtual education, UWI introduced its Open Campus. This is a virtual campus with over 40 physical site locations across the region and serves over 16 countries in the English-speaking Caribbean. More high school graduates have an opportunity to enroll at UWI with online course offerings,

UWI's Mona Campus continues to maintain its premier standing throughout the Caribbean. In response to the changing times, the institution consistently expands its academic offerings for undergraduate, masters, and doctoral programs in humanities and education, science and technology, science and agriculture, engineering, law, medical sciences and social sciences. Intramural and extramural sports have also become an important aspect of the university's offerings. These activities allow students to compete among themselves and other post-secondary institutions.

Stewart Town
Trelawny Parish

Stewart Town was established in 1815 and is located adjacent to Trelawny's eastern border with the St Ann's parish. It was not established as a free village, but it steadily evolved into one of the free villages where farmers and merchants would flock weekly to sell their goods to the bustling crowd of people. Stewart Town was named after plantation owner, James Stewart, who was instrumental in its establishment. Stewart's estate began as a small 167-acre landholding but by 1799, slave labor was instrumental in the sugar plantation's expansion to over 1200 acres. The town is also known for the Stewart Castle, the mansion of James Stewart that was built by his slaves. The castle was surrounded by well-fortified walls to guard against attacks from escaped, armed Maroons. The walls also prevented Maroons from interacting with 300 slaves within the fort, which stopped the slaves from participating in any rebellions. Stewart Town has lost its popularity and is now a quiet little district with many old buildings and ruins that include Stewart Castle.

Westwood High School for Girls was established because of long-standing racial prejudices that prevailed against the rights of Jamaican children to obtain an education equal to children of the white ruling class. Two ladies from the famous William Knibb family operated The Ms. Knibb's Young Ladies' Seminary that catered to both boarding and day-school students in the rural town of Falmouth, the capital of the parish of Trelawny. The town was a central, prosperous hub during the slave trade due to its many sugar plantations, but its economy declined after emancipation. The Knibb women decided to break the tradition of primarily enrolling girls from the ruling class family, so they accepted two Jamaican girls, the daughters of well-known ministers in the community. When white parents learned of the two new students, they demanded for the Knibbs to expel both. However, when the ladies refused to comply with this order, the white parents withdrew their daughters from the school. During that period, Rev. Webb, a Baptist minister, recognized a need to open a school for Jamaican girls in the community. His efforts to gain support in England failed, so he eventually partnered with Rev. Henderson, another Baptist minister to make the goal a reality. They leased a house near Stewart Town and opened a school with one teacher and six girls in 1880 (Ogilvie, n.d.). It was known as The Manchester Girls' School, but the name was changed to The Trelawny Girls' School to identify with the parish where it was located. Many girls began to enroll, and with the rapid increase in the student population, it was necessary to secure a larger, permanent location. Rev. Webb and Rev. Henderson gained the support of the Ladies in England to secure funding to purchase property and construct a building at a total cost of approximately £3,000 (Ogilvie, n.d.). Construction was completed in 1895, and the move to better accommodations brought more stability. This expansion and the school's good reputation were factors that caused it to begin obtaining applications from prospective students throughout different parts of the island. The name was changed to Westwood High School since the institution was no longer only identifiable with students from Trelawny, but it also accepted girls from different parts of Jamaica. Ogilvie (n.d.) reports that a trust deed was established to make the school nondenominational. Four Jamaican trustees representing the Baptist, Anglican, Wesleyan and Presbyterian churches were appointed by the Ladies in England. They also assumed the responsibility of selecting the English headmistress. By 1913, the Ladies in England ended their financial support. At that time, however, the school had been established into a sound educational institution. It eventually became a government run institution.

Today, Westwood High School is one of the two remaining boarding schools for girls in Jamaica. Westwood also boasts the immaculately clad appearance of their students. It is the only girls' school that has continued the colonial tradition where girls are expected to wear hats. The jippy-jappy hats enhance the style of the students' basic navy-blue uniform that would otherwise go unnoticed. The girls' school is also consistently one of the top academic-performing secondary schools in Jamaica. It has produced throughout the years many scholars who have made a positive impression on young girls not only at Westwood High School but others throughout the country.

Denbigh
Clarendon Parish

Penrhyn Estate, Denbigh, was one of the largest sugar plantations in rural Jamaica. It was owned by the absentee Pennant family. The majority of the family's slaves were assigned to the Penrhyn Estate and the others worked on their five other plantations (SocialistWorker, n.d). The family dominated the slave trade from the beginning of slavery up until its abolition when they defended the need to maintain slavery. Their support to maintain slavery was not surprising because their participation in every aspect of the business allowed them to become wealthy and the owners of the Penrhyn Estate. The family's accumulated wealth over the years from their plantations also enabled ownership of the enormous Penrhyn Castle in Wales.

The town of Denbigh consists of a parcel of land from the Penrhyn Estate. It remains primarily a farming town where the Denbigh Agricultural and Industrial Show is held. This is the oldest and largest agricultural show in the English-speaking Caribbean. It is a well-attended three-day event that attracts from 60,000 to 80,000 visitors at the Denbigh Show Ground. The Denbigh Show has been embedded in the Jamaican culture from 1953 to present. The annual show is a highlight of what the country has achieved in agriculture and its related sectors. Farmers showcase their livelihood such as their finest quality agricultural produces, livestock, and culinary products. This hallmark event has brought popularity to the community.

Denbigh High School

Denbigh High School was opened in the rural town of its name sake. Its opening has ensured that students have an opportunity to be educated beyond the primary school level. The school has been classified as one of the best upgraded secondary schools in Jamaica. Their performance is in contrast to the lack of academic progress of other upgraded secondary schools that continue to lag behind traditional secondary schools. Similar to other new secondary schools, Denbigh High School experienced several name changes, from junior secondary school, to secondary school in 1974, then comprehensive high in 1995, and finally to high school in 2000. The institution opened in 1966 with 810 students who transitioned from feeder primary schools around the community. The school's high pass rate on the Grade 9 Achievement Test enabled students to transfer to a traditional secondary school. However, grades 10 and 11 were added to meet the demand of those who were not successful at the Grade 9 Achievement Test. A two-shift system was implemented to accommodate the over 1,000 student population. But, during the late 70s to early 80s, high standards, student attendance, academic achievement, discipline and even school maintenance began to decline. Low enrollment of fewer than 300 students justified the school's need to return to the single shift system.

A turn-around of the school began as administration, students, parents, corporate entities and the community worked together to correct the problems that plagued the institution for years. Changes involved erecting a well-needed perimeter fence; using the talents of agricultural students to beautify the campus; repairing broken and dilapidated infrastructure; providing a tuck shop to generate income; and adding newly constructed buildings. The curriculum was expanded to include science subjects to give more academic opportunities for the incoming class of students including those who entered grade 7 in 1995 after passing the Common Entrance Exam. Enrollment returned to an all-time high of 1500 students.

Denbigh High School outshined other upgraded secondary schools in the past and received a number one ranking among those schools in mathematics and English on the CXC exams. A grade 12 program was started at the school, and it also received a number one ranking among the upgraded secondary schools. Such accomplishments are generally expected from students at the traditional secondary schools, so Denbigh High School is making a name for itself as it continues to achieve high standards.

Trinidad & Tobago
Education During and After Slavery

Public schools for slaves were non-existent in Trinidad and Tobago prior to emancipation. Unlike other Caribbean territories, wealthy merchants and planters did not provide endowments or charity to fund public schools where poor white boys or even free biracial children from elite families could attend (Campbell, 1996). Missionaries also made no attempt to teach literacy to small groups of slaves as their counterparts in other Caribbean islands. Once slavery was abolished, education for the majority population was not a priority for the government. Their social and political concerns delayed their participation in the timely construction of primary schools to accommodate freed children. Religious organizations, however, recognized the need and dominated the educational system during the initial stages after emancipation by opening primary schools throughout the island with grant-in-aid financial incentives provided to them by the government. These denominational organizations continued their dominance of the primary education system even after the financial incentives from the government decreased. When the state considered the educational needs of the majority population, they used Mico Charity funds along with grant-in-aid to build 30 primary schools.

In 1836, funds primarily from the Negro Education grant with limited government financial resources enabled the construction of the first post-elementary, non-denominational school, where ex-slaves and the biracial population could attend. The training school closed around 1845, but in 1852, another post-elementary training school, was opened to non-whites. Enrollment was limited at both training schools. So, the institutions could not accept many who wanted to continue their education after completing elementary school at age 14 years.

During the mid-19th century, the government funded the construction of the first state secondary school in the country. However, this public school was opened to the white students and a limited number of biracial students but not Afro-Trinidadians. Even if Afro-Trinidadians had outstanding academic abilities, they would be denied based on various excuses such as their illegitimate birth status. This denial of their enrollment signaled that secondary education was a privilege for only a small segment of the population (The History of Secondary Education and the Development of Curricula, n.d.). The next public secondary school was constructed a century after the opening of the first. Enrollment for Afro-Trinidadians changed for a few students years later when they gained acceptance at elite public secondary institutions based on their outstanding performances on exams such as the College Exhibition Examination.

Tobago

Tobago was considered a slave society. In 1790 the population was primarily African slaves. As a result of slave labor, Tobago prospered economically for the first three decades of the nineteenth century. Even after the abolition of the slave trade in 1807, the high birth rate of slaves continued to provide Tobago's plantations with sufficient labor. The Emancipation Act of 1834 did not result in total freedom for the slaves until 1838. At that time, the Tobago Abolition Act was enforced which specified that estate owners must provide ex-slaves with small plots for their own cultivation. So, a large number of ex-slaves became peasant farmers. They grew primarily ground provisions and also reared goats, sheep, and poultry. But others continued to work on estates as hired laborers. Men were paid one shilling a day while women received eight pence a day.

After slavery, the Anglican, Methodist, Moravian, and later the Roman Catholic churches took the responsibility of opening primary schools since the government did not become actively involved in providing elementary education to the population of Tobago until during the 20th century. Even today, government-run free primary schools are limited in comparison to the many primary schools that are associated with the church which operates them with some government assistance. However, the government is fully responsible for secondary education that is free of costs to students.

The population of Tobago is primarily of African descent. As reported on the 2011 census, 60,874 resided on the island. Its capital, Scarborough, has a population of 17,537. The island celebrates a number of cultural events throughout the year, but the biggest annual event is the "Bago Carnival" that takes place in February when the streets are filled with masquerade bands. Residents wear glistening outfits as they dance to the rhythm of calypso and soca music. They eat Creole foods that symbolizes their culture from the slavery era.

Bishop's High School

Bishop's High School is Tobago's oldest secondary educational institution. Tobago's former slaves and their descendants did not have opportunities to attend a secondary school for decades until the co-educational Anglican school was opened on September 14th, 1925 in Scarborough. The cost to attend the school was initially not free, so parents made sacrifices to obtain funds to pay the school fees so that their children could continue with their education. By 1928 only 44 students were enrolled, so Bishop's High School was considered the smallest of the twin island's secondary schools. The critics in Trinidad believed that only a limited number of students qualified for secondary education in Tobago. However, the people of Tobago were more concerned that they finally had a secondary school that would accept their children which was contrary to secondary schools in Trinidad.

One major turning point for the school was its relocation to more spacious premises which enabled the introduction of other courses such as science. However, recruiting teacher to work at the new campus was a challenge since teachers from Trinidad were reluctant to relocate to work in Tobago during the early 1960s. Consequently, the school relied on recruiting teachers from England and Barbados. The school made all efforts to avoid such staffing problems from recurring by training their own Tobago graduates as teachers. They were offered government scholarships and private donations from benefactors. By the 1980s, approximately 75 percent of the staff at Bishop's High School were Tobagonians.

According to Campbell (1997), the opening of the school signified the beginning of the Afro-Trinidadian middle class. The institution has been known throughout the years for the upward mobility of students from poor background into the middle-management professions and life-styles. In spite of earlier doubts, the institution has emerged as one of the top secondary schools in the twin island.

Roxborough Secondary School
and
Signal Hill Secondary School

One of the most significant events in the history of Trinidad and Tobago occurred on January 16th, 1961, when five free secondary schools were opened. Scarborough Secondary School was one of those schools, and the first of its kind to be established in Tobago. Thereafter, Roxborough Secondary School was opened with 160 students and 20 staff members in 1965. Later, Signal Hill Secondary School was opened initially as a comprehensive school in 1977 with 120 fourth form or grade 10 students who were transferred from Roxborough and Scarborough secondary schools. These secondary schools in Tobago met the placement needs of poor children who finally had the opportunity to obtain post-elementary education instead of ending their learning after completing primary school. At first, many parents preferred to send their children to Bishop's High School, the traditional secondary school. Their belief was that the colonial system of education at Bishop's High School was better than the new educational system at the modern secondary schools. But parents had to accept that only those students with high achievement scores on the Common Entrance Exam would be placed at Bishop's High School. Subjects taught at the new secondary schools have included academic courses in addition to vocational courses such as technical drawing, clothing and textile, woodwork, beauty culture, food and nutrition. The new secondary schools have encountered challenges throughout the years, but they have continued to overcome some of these struggles. Student achievement has steadily improved on the Caribbean Examinations Council (CXC), the high school exit exams.

University of the West Indies,
University of Trinidad and Tobago,
and
College of Science, Technology, and Applied Arts

Post-secondary education was not available on the island of Tobago until as late as the 21st century. Although the University of the West Indies (UWI) opened the St. Augustine Campus in Trinidad during the 1960s, outstanding students in Tobago who possessed the criteria to attend UWI had to relocate to Trinidad if they wanted to attend the university. UWI eventually followed the trend of universities worldwide by expanding its enrollment to include those registering for open campus and online learning courses. This modern learning concept allowed students in Tobago to enroll in UWI's distance learning, online, or blended courses.

The University of Trinidad and Tobago (UTT) launched a campus in Tobago in 2013. The primary intention was to address the teacher shortage by providing courses in education. Students enrolled in programs work towards obtaining bachelor's degrees in education. Experienced teachers may enroll in higher education degree programs or take professional development courses at UTT. The university accepts full or part-time students in programs such as Primary Education, Early Childhood Care and Primary Education, or Special Needs and Primary Education.

College of Science, Technology, and Applied Arts of Trinidad & Tobago (COSTAATT), the national community college, established a center in Tobago during this 21st century. In doing so, the college continues to meet its expectations of addressing the needs of the residents by providing access to socially relevant and innovative educational programs that will benefit single parents, part-time or temporary workers, students from underserved communities, and secondary-school leavers. Students enroll in a two-year program to obtain an associate degree, but they also have access to bachelor's degree programs. Courses include early childhood care and education, nursing, business administration, and mass communications. COSTAATT also provides infrastructure and equipped classrooms where programs are offered using distance learning technology via the internet.

Barbados
Education During and After Slavery

Attempts were made to educate slaves and their children in 1818, when a school was built in Bridgetown to provide biracial boys with an elementary education. Several informal day schools were opened and almost every Barbadian parish began a Sunday school that was intended for the slave population (Blouet, 1980). Some estate owners also allowed informal instructions on their plantations. The actions were in total contrast to the opinions of earlier planters about not educating slaves. On the other hand, white parents who could afford the expenses sent their sons to England to be educated in upper-class schools and universities. Lower income white children attended charity schools that were founded prior to the abolition of slavery. Those schools were associated with the estate of Colonel Drax at Constitution Road; Captain Francis Williams in Christ Church; and Christopher Codrington in St. John.

In 1934 after emancipation, several schools were started for ex-slaves on church premises and taught by those former slaves who could read and write or by the clergy. Estate schools were also setup to provide education to those who worked as apprentices on properties. These schools provided elementary level education and apprenticeship programs. Thereafter, the school board realized the need for mass primary education as a means to maintain control of the Afro-Barbadian population. But some parents could not afford to send their children to those primary school because of the weekly school fees.

Secondary education was only considered for the British and a few privilege biracial children. Layne (2002) confirms that the promotion of mass primary education as an instrument of social control while reserving secondary education for a fortunate few continued to be the defining features of educational policies in Barbados up until the 20th century. So, very little was done by the government to provide students with post-elementary education more than a half century after the passage of the1833 Act of Emancipation. In 1932, the masses of Afro-Barbadian students had more opportunities to attend elite secondary schools. However, an obstacle was that fees ranged from £5 to £15 per annum, which was well above the amount parents of limited income could afford. So, by the end of World War II, the secondary school system in Barbados remained as exclusive as ever.

Bridgetown
St. Michael's Parish

Bridgetown, the capital city of Barbados, was founded by the British during the early 17th century. Its port was fortified and known not only as a popular trading post for goods such as sugar, but it was often the first port of call for ships overcrowded with slaves who were transported from Africa through the Transatlantic Passage to their final destinations. Bridgetown became a center where slaves were sold and distributed throughout the Americas after they disembarked the vessels. Bridgetown developed into Britain's most profitable port, so it was considered a prized possession of the crown for nearly three centuries.

Bridgetown is known for its Crop Over celebrations. Crop Over, formerly known as Harvest Home, is an annual tradition in Barbados that began in 1687 on the sugar plantations during slavery to celebrate the end of the sugar cane crop. The end of the harvest meant the end of many long months of hard labor on over 500 plantations. At that time, the parade featured carts decorated with flowers to depict the last of the season's crops that were brought into the mill yard. The first cart was led by a woman in a white dress which is now equivalent to the frontline dancers in the modern-day street parade. The woman used to be accompanied by various sugar cane workers all carrying the final loads of canes. The last cart depicted an effigy of "Mr. Harding" to represent the hard times for slaves from the end of the sugar crop season to the beginning of the next season. The parade would end with the burning of 'Mr. Harding' to symbolize hope that the hard times would not be too rough. The Crop Over Festival has since become Barbados' biggest national festival.

St. Leonard's Boys Secondary School

St. Leonard's Boys Secondary School was the first government free secondary school. It was opened in 1952 more than a century after the abolition of slavery. This and other schools thereafter were built under the recommendation of the Mayhew Commission's 1932 report that included the need to introduce the "modern" secondary school since other secondary schools' elite enrollment practices did not give the majority population much opportunity to expand knowledge past grade school. Even if some low-income, working-class parents could afford the nominal fees to send their child to an elite school, they would have to pay additional fees at the secondary school. This was unaffordable for many whose children had to leave school at 14 years old. Therefore, the government's opening of St. Leonard's provided hope to many poor parents who could not afford for their children to progress beyond the primary school level. St. Leonard's Boys Secondary School brought more stability to continuing a secondary education past 14 years old. The Mayhew Commission report also resulted in the opening of St. Leonard's Girls Secondary School, the second modern school. Opened during the same year as the boys' school, this free secondary girls' school provided educational opportunities mainly for girls from low income homes who would have to resort to domestic duties instead of continuing their education. However, the girls' school did not fear as well as the boys' school since it was closed in 1997.

Initially, in addition to teaching the customary academic subjects, students at the boys' and girls' new secondary schools had the opportunity to gain knowledge in practical courses such as domestic science, book binding, woodwork and metalwork. By 1962, the steady growth of students at the boys' school resulted in a need for a shift system and expansion of the facilities. In 1964 St. Leonard's Boys' School became a comprehensive school with an emphasis on technical subjects with some vocational and academic classes.

St. Leonard's Boys School has become one of the outstanding schools on the island. The school has maintained a one shift system where it offers students a comprehensive selection of classes ranging from general studies to industrial arts. It is one of the few secondary schools that offer a 6th form or grade 12 education. The school's 100 boys' choir is the first of its kind in Barbados and has become well known on the island.

Erdiston Teachers' Training College

A teacher training institution was not established on the island in a timely manner after emancipation to address primary school instructional needs. The closest teacher training institution to Barbados was a women's normal college in Antigua. Final year students attending primary school who were interested in becoming teachers in Barbados would have to be considered by their teachers to assist them in the classroom to gain teaching experience. Then, Rawle Teacher Training Institute was opened in 1912. This affiliate of Codrington College closed after Erdiston Teacher Training College was established in 1948 with 32 students. The institution initially offered a one-year program in subjects such as English, math, religion, home economics, music and other subjects. The population increased rapidly by 1954 with students enrolled not only from Barbados but also from other eastern Caribbean countries such as Grenada, St. Lucia, Montserrat, Dominica and Tortola. After University College of the West Indies' Cave Hill (UWI) campus opened in Barbados in 1963, Erdiston Teacher Training College formed a partnership with the university's School of Education in 1964. Throughout the years, the college has expanded its offerings by providing teach-the-teacher training programs; continuing education for professional development in administrative areas; teacher certified programs; vocational technical programs; computer-based programs; continued professional education; and other new programs. The college has withstood difficult times and continues to introduce new programs including Bachelor of Education degree programs along with a Diploma in Education Leadership program. The college has also incorporated the new age of computers into training teachers. Furthermore, the novel methods of learning have influenced the college to adapt some of its course deliveries to open college, online format, or blended mode. Performance based assessment has also outweighed the former pen and paper test taking method.

The Samuel Jackman Prescod Institute of Technology

Since 1969, Samuel Jackman Prescod Institute of Technology has been an option for students interested in continuing their education in technical and vocational courses that will lead directly to careers. Courses include agriculture, car mechanics, architectural drafting, welding, plumbing, hairdressing, and catering. Originally known as the Samuel Jackman Prescod Polytechnic, it expanded through its merger with the Barbados Technical Institute in 1972. Further expansions occurred in 1975 with its merger with the Division of Agriculture. In addition to its own programs, the polytechnic also provides training for the Barbados Vocational Training Board which operates a number of centers throughout the island to provide skills training programs, apprenticeship programs, and in-plant programs. Moreover, their training programs extend to secondary school students, industrial workers and teachers. On October 19th, 2017, the Samuel Jackman Prescod Polytechnic was officially renamed the Samuel Jackman Prescod Institute of Technology.

Barbados Community College

The Barbados Community College (BCC) was established by an Act of Parliament in 1968. Many secondary school graduates who applied to the University of the West Indies' (UWI), Cave Hill Campus were denied due to the highly selective admissions' requirements. So, Barbados Community College became an option for students because the institution accepted a wide cross-section of the population with less stringent academic requirements than UWI. The first class included 325 students. Enrollment has increased steadily throughout the years to approximately 3,000. The institution continues to grant certificates, diplomas, associate degrees, bachelor's degrees and other awards to persons who have successfully completed courses of study approved by the Board of Management. The college was initially established to provide classes in agriculture, commerce, fine arts, liberal arts, science and technology. These courses and others have been

streamlined into departments that include Health Sciences,
Computer Studies, Physical Education, the Language
Centre, Hospitality Studies, and Continuing Education.

Guyana
Education During and After Slavery

Planters in Guyana were more interested in putting the slave labor force to work on the plantations, so educating them was not a priority. However, under both the Dutch and British colonial systems, religious organizations offered informal schooling to teach slaves about the qualities of spiritual and moral goodness. Planters were fearful that obtaining an education would incite slaves to revolt and stop working on the plantations. So, they strongly resisted the education of slaves especially after the 1823 slavery revolt. However, the church organizations continued with their unstructured teaching efforts (Mangar, 2009). The Anglicans opened two informal schools - St. George's Free School in 1824 and All Saints School in 1829.

After the abolition of slavery in 1834, public education was affected by a number of factors that included: low government priority; inadequate funding; teacher shortage; parents' resistance due to perceptions of a flawed system; and unaffordable school fees (Mangar, 2009). Furthermore, the formal system of education provided in primary schools was implemented on the basis of teaching certain subjects that would cause the ex-slaves to remain submissive.

In 1844, the first government secondary school, Queen's College, was established. Mangar (2009) reports that the school was opened only to those whites whose parents could not afford to send them for schooling in England. For a non-white boy to enter, he had to be exceptionally gifted as was the case four years later when two Afro-Guyanese boys were considered for entry. These students were accepted on an experimental basis only. Their academic successes opened the door for those Afro-Guyanese and biracial students, who could afford the fees and were also academically outstanding. By placing such restrictions to prevent the laboring class from attending a public secondary school, the British government demonstrated their narrow-minded thinking that the majority population had no ability to learn beyond basic education.

Proprietary Villages

After emancipation, slaves were required to work without income through an apprenticeship program up until 1838. Many planters did not agree with the policy of the British government to make former slaves free laborers who made their own decisions after the completion of their apprenticeship. The planters believed with complete freedom, the former apprentices would abandon the estates which would lead to a labor shortage and the collapse of the sugar industry. So, they made all effort to oversee the system by implementing measures to control former apprentices. On the other hand, some planters were not concerned with the British policies. These planters expected former apprentices to remain on plantations to work the land because they would continue to have free housing which would ease financial burdens if they did not earn enough from their crops to cover their other expenses. So, many former apprentices continued to work on the plantations. Others wanted to be regarded as free men and show their independence by leaving the plantations on which they had endured so much humiliation and sufferings. Some of these men and women pooled their money together and purchased estates that were abandoned. This was the start of the proprietary village system where former slaves purchased land and worked together to develop the necessary infrastructures to make a livable community for all dwellers. The financial benefits that generated from selling land to former slaves led other planters to follow. By the end of 1841, planters were offering lands for sale or lease, and the practice quickly spread. By the end of 1848 only approximately 19,939 laborers remained on the sugar estates while an estimated 44,556 resided in proprietary villages (McAlmont McAlmont, 2013). It was not easy for these new landowners since some unscrupulous white planters tried to force them to abandon the land after taking their money. Furthermore, they had to deal with limited finances to maintain existing infrastructure. Moreover, the new land owners were initially unfamiliar with procedures to maintain a communal village.

Golden Grove Village
East Coast Demerara
Mahaica-Berbice Region

On January 5, 1848, 50 men pooled their resources and bought Plantation Williamsburg, an abandoned sugar estate. Soon after the purchase, the name Williamsburg was changed to Golden Grove. Two years after the purchase, a survey of the newly-acquired settlement was made, and the land was divided into residential lots and agricultural land. Houses were built on stilts and assembled on both sides of the public road and internal streets. Small two to three acres farms were scattered throughout the backlands. Throughout the 1850s, villagers travelled each day from their homes to their farms and back either by boat along the canals or by foot over the dams. Golden Grove became a village in 1892, and the village council was established. Most of the descendants of former African slaves have continued to reside in Golden Grove Village, so they make up the majority of the population. Farming remains the major source of income for most residents.

President's College

President's College was established as a boarding school on September 11, 1985 by Guyana's first Executive President, the late Linden Forbes Burnham. Seventy-two students were selected from the top 2 percent of candidates from the Secondary School Entrance Examination (SSEE). They also completed an evaluation and interview. President Burnham was concerned with the nation's continued focus on past achievements and through education, he wanted to provide possibilities for new accomplishments. President Burnham did not live to see the inauguration of the school. However, on the school's opening, the new president of Guyana reiterated President Burnham's vision that President's College was for gifted children, but it would not adapt the old, unjust system that catered primarily to children of the elite and disregarded underserved students. In the president's speech, the main concept instilled in the minds of many was that President's College was built by the people for the people as a result of their contributions in making the school a reality in Golden Grove Village.

President's College started on a high note, and the school eventually became one of the top five schools in Guyana. However, it has undergone challenges, which included a fire that destroyed the boys' dorm. The school has also been impacted by the lack of well-maintained buildings, a common problem that affects schools located in rural communities. In spite of the difficulties, the school continues to be known for its high academic standards. The enrollment polices are now open to students who live anywhere in Guyana. However, preference is still given to those residing in Golden Grove Village, the surrounding communities, and other remote areas. Dormitory accommodations continue to be available to students, but

President's College now also functions also as a day school for those students who commute from their homes.

Buxton Village
Demerara
Mahaica-Berbice Region

Buxton was regarded as Guyana's premier village of the colony due to its size and value (Tyrrell-Kellman, n.d.). The 580-acre plantation was purchased in 1840 after emancipation and apprenticeship. The village was developed into the largest and one of the most efficient local authorities in the country. Friendship, its sister village of 700 acres was founded in 1841 by former slaves. Buxton and Friendship villages were later joined to form the village of Buxton-Friendship, which is commonly called Buxton. After an initial period of difficulties, the villagers formed their own government by establishing the Buxton-Friendship Local Authority to manage their own community's affairs. The council made lands available for the construction of housing, schools, churches, drainage, and other infrastructure. These former slaves also designated large areas of lands for farming cash crops. In 1856, the British Guiana Legislature authorized the government to pass improvement taxes on the properties of the villagers. This led to a standoff between the government and the purchasers of Buxton. Lengthy impasses and actions of perceived betrayal lead he residents to block the train carrying the governor. He subsequently exempted all from paying taxes. The Buxton community has significantly contributed to the preservation of African culture in Guyana. Each year, the community organizes a week of activities to celebrate Emancipation Day on August 1st. The village has experienced challenges with poverty and crime throughout the years, but it continues to be known for its historic accomplishments.

Buxton Secondary School

Buxton-Friendship Local Authority realized that very few of its residents could read or write, so building schools was a priority. (Tyrrell-Kellman, n.d.). They focused on this issue by setting aside land to construct elementary schools. Students who completed elementary school and wanted to continue their education had to go to secondary schools in Georgetown, the capital city or to the commercial school in Beterverwagting. Decades later, three secondary schools were built in the village. However, Buxton Secondary School is the only one that remains after the closure of the other two institutions. Buxton Secondary School is considered a low tiered school that has served as a feeder for those primary school students who had not performed successfully on the National Grade Six Assessment to attend a traditional secondary school. The school property was used not only for classes but also for school concerts, school sports, and 'Open Days' when the parents and residents were invited to see the work of students. During earlier years, the school also played an important role in the social development of the village. It catered to residents who wanted continuing education courses to learn domestic skills such as cooking, sewing, and gardening.

The Buxton Practical Instruction Centre (PIC) provides pre-vocational education and skills training to children and adults in areas such as agricultural science, computer science, garment construction, woodworks, joinery, home economics, and catering. The center was opened in September 2010 and is one of approximately 12 similar institutes throughout Guyana. The staff of 13 teachers also work together with teachers at the Buxton Secondary School to prepare students for the Secondary Competency

Certificate Programme (SCCP) and the Caribbean Secondary Education Certificate (CSEC).

Georgetown
Demerara-Mahaica Region

The city of Georgetown began as a small town during the 18th century. When the British seized the coastal and internal region from the first Dutch occupiers, they founded the settlement. However, the French captured the region one year later from the British. The French developed and named the settlement, La Nouvelle Ville and declared it the capital of their colony. After the Dutch reclaimed the region, they renamed the settlement Stabroek. In 1796, Britain established permanent control of the colony. In 1812 Stabroek became known as Georgetown in honor of King George III. It was later declared the capital of the colony of British Guiana in 1831.

During the initial settlement of the Dutch, they imported slaves to work on the sugar plantations in regions that included their prized Georgetown settlement. A second batch of an influx of slaves arrived when additional acreage was added to Georgetown to include estates such as Vlissingen, La Bourgade, Eve Leary, Werk-en-rust and La Repentir. Many emancipated slaves from countryside plantations flocked to Georgetown and greatly increased the town's population. Today, Afro-Guyanese represents approximately 30 percent of the population of Georgetown.

February is designated as African History Month. During this month, emphasis is placed on performing arts activities that are associated with the African culture. The Emancipation Day celebrations are held every August. During the celebrations, there are many exhibitions which include those at the Emancipation Festival at the National

Park. Patrons enjoy viewing demonstrations of folk and village games along with exhibitions. Guests also show their appreciation for craftwork, paintings, performances and many more activities in celebration of the end of slavery.

Government Technical Institute

The Government Technical Institute (GTI) opened its doors in 1951 with 150 students. The intentions to open a technical school were to provide an option for those students leaving high school who wanted to gain employment skills that would lead to careers. Furthermore, GTI was the next best option for those students who may have wanted to attend the University of Guyana but did not achieve the academic requirements. Initially, students enrolled in day or night programs received instructions in craft skills only. But, by 1956, the institution offered technical level courses. Further course expansions were introduced in 1961, and students enrolled in diploma courses. Students can now choose from a variety of technical programs that are administered in one of the school's seven departments that include: Building Department, Electrical Department, Mechanical Department, Business Department, Science Department, Information Technology Department, and Land and Surveying Department. Today, the school's enrollment has increased to approximately 2,000 full and part-time students with a large population of Afro-Guyanese learners.

In spite of the continued growth and successes of GTI, the institution maintains a stigma as a school for low achievers especially in the areas of math and English language proficiency. Therefore, most high achievers are not expected to attend GTI but the University of Guyana instead. However, GTI has laid the foundation even for high achievers. Some of those students prefer to transfer from high school to GTI where they can acquire practical skills that will enable them to gain employment.

Cyril Potter College of Education

Cyril Potter College of Education was established in September 1928. The institution became an option for those Afro-Guyanese who wanted to become teachers but could not afford to relocate to other countries to attend institutions such as Mico College in Antigua, Shortwood College in Jamaica, and Rawle College in Barbados. Initially, the teacher's college was known as Teachers' Training Centre (TTC). The institution was renamed Government Training College for teachers (GTC) in 1942. During the early years, trainees were expected to enroll in a full-time program, but in 1963, they had the option of registering for part-time studies. The full-time program or pre-service program catered to younger post-secondary students from 17 to 24 years old while the part-time program or in-service program was opened to those 24 years old and older who already possessed relevant teaching experiences. By 1969, secondary program was implemented to address a need for secondary school teachers. Now, the college offers a two-year program for those who want to teach nursery and primary school and a three years program for those who prefer to teach at the secondary or vocational school levels. Graduates are expected to serve as government teacher for five years. Afro-Guyanese teachers who live and teach in rural areas may upgrade their instructional skills by attending off-campus programs offered by the teachers' college in their communities.

Tain, Berbice
East Berbice-Corentyne Region

Berbice, a region along the Berbice River in Guyana, was a colony of the Netherlands from 1627 to 1815. Berbice is significant to the Afro-Guyanese population since it was the location of slave plantations such as Blairmont, Balthyock, Canefield, Everton, Friends, Providence and Rose Hall. Berbice is also recognized for the Berbice slave uprising that was organized and led by Cuffy in 1763. The slaves were defeated due to splits in the rebel leadership and the arrival of Dutch reinforcements. The United Kingdom eventually gained control of the colony, and it merged with Essequibo and Demerara to form the colony of British Guiana in 1831.

University of Guyana - Tain/Berbice Campus

Centuries after emancipation, graduates of secondary schools did not have access to enrolling in degree programs at a local university. Some completed post-secondary diploma programs instead at Government Technical Institute and Guyana Industrial Training Centre. But those families who could afford to, sent their children abroad to continue their education. The lack of a local university continued until 1963 when the University of Guyana was established. Approximately 164 students enrolled at temporary facilities on the Queen's College campus until the university's Turkeyen Campus was opened in Georgetown. The university was initially operated as an evening institution but expanded significantly on a full-time basis by offerings a wide range of diploma and degree programs.

The University of Guyana opened the Tain campus in 2000. This second campus has provided a well-needed location for those Afro-Guyanese students residing in rural villages and/or settlements in Berbice and elsewhere. Prior to the opening, students had to travel long distances to attend the main campus in Georgetown. In addition to offering a number of academic programs, collaborative programs are provided to enhance the lives of people residing in rural communities. For instance, social work final year students built a shade house for secondary school students to use as part of their farming activities. The university also provided farmers with an opportunity to be trained and certified in crop protection. The signing of a $40 million Memorandum of Understanding to construct a soil testing facility is another example of continued commitment to the development of the community. This has allowed the Tain Campus students to partner with farmers in soil testing and disease projects.

The Other Caribbean Journey

French Caribbean Territories and Education

The French were the third largest slave traders based on the 773,000 majority of Africans delivered to Saint-Domingue (Haiti) during the late 18th century which was almost double the number of Africans transported to North America. The second largest delivery, 217,200 slaves, was sent to Martinique. Guadeloupe received 73,000 slaves, and others were transported to French Guiana. Haiti's sugar plantations remained France's crown jewel until the Haitian Revolution in 1791. Haitians fought bravely against the French army to gain their independence. They became the first colony to secure their freedom from an oppressive French regime and planter class. The French government subsequently abolished slavery in Martinique, Guadeloupe, and French Guiana after the 1848 revolution that caused slave uprisings throughout the colonies.

The French Colonial Ordinance of 1685, also known as the "Black Code", included 60 articles that regulated the life, death, purchase, religion, and treatment of slaves in all French colonies. The ordinance included that the slaves should be baptized and educated in the Catholic faith. In some French Caribbean countries, a handful of children of privileged slaves began to attend part-time schools. Eventually, the idea of schools for slaves was allowed by liberal French metropolitan governments during the early 19th century. Slaves could immediately attend school after emancipation because there were no apprenticeship laws. However, anyone wishing to send their children over the age of 12 to school was required to pay a tax. Also, after emancipation, the French government approved the funding and development of a public educational system in its colonies to provide the majority population with primary schools where they could learn writing and arithmetic. On behalf of the French government, the Boards of Education conducted regular inspections and control of the schools. Local governments throughout the French Caribbean islands formed partnerships with churches to offer primary school education. The foremost intention of the governments in offering education to the marginalized groups was to maintain their subordination and continued economic productions rather than to provide them with a way to progress out of their low-level status.

In Haiti, Martinique, and Guadeloupe the curriculum at secondary high schools modeled the syllabus in France. Aspiring people of African heritage and the biracial population welcomed the connections that would allow them to maintain a close relationship to secondary schools in France.

Haiti
Education During and After Slavery

Saint-Domingue became independent in 1804, and its name was changed to Haiti. Prior to independence, children of planters and merchants were educated at home and sent to France to continue their education. The brutal, oppressive system created by the white planters and merchants gave no consideration to educating slaves. Those who were found educating slaves would have to pay substantial penalties. Planters were of the impression that educating slaves would cause them to challenge authority and rebel. So, they felt that in their best interest, it was better to keep slaves ignorant. On the other hand, some slaveholders recognized the benefits of slaves gaining knowledge to take on other responsibilities besides working on the land. This optimism allowed slaves, such as Toussaint Louverture, to receive an education that eventually led to their national leadership roles.

Despite Haiti becoming an independent nation, education of former slaves did not progress as expected because they were confined to lower educational standards. Haitians did not have the privilege of obtaining the high-level education offered to biracial residents who formed an elite class. The biracial group learned in French, and they maintained a commitment to maintaining the French language and culture. But the majority population were shut-out from making progress because they were not taught the French language. A structural elementary system of education or strategy to consider methods of educating the majority population was not even considered under the governorship of Toussaint Louverture. In fact, many of the leaders of Haiti's independence were illiterate.

The declaration made in the Constitution of 1816 for free primary education was not implemented due to a lack of funds and the scarcity of trained teachers. Yet, the government found resources to establish Lycee Alexandre Petion, a public secondary school in 1816 for the elite class. So, Haitian leaders were guilty of implementing similar harsh practices as their predecessors by denying their disenfranchised countrymen the right to basic education.

At the end of the 19th century, there were 350 public schools in the country, and the majority were primary schools. But, children from low income backgrounds could not afford to attend the government schools because they would have to pay fees and extra costs for school uniforms, shoes, textbooks, and other expenses. So, the system at that time was still not meant to educate the average Haitian who spoke Haitian Creole and not French, the language of instruction. By the beginning of the 20th century, only approximately 10 percent of secondary schools were government run. Throughout the years, Haiti has remained the Western Hemisphere country with the highest illiteracy rate. The 2010 earthquake aggravated the situation when over 4,000 schools were severely damaged or completely destroyed. Through international aid programs and non-profit organizations, government schools were rebuilt, and some new secondary schools were opened in rural communities where children had no access to post-elementary education.

Those Haitian children who do not attend school, for various reasons, face a life of poverty and illiteracy. On the other hand, the lives of those who can afford to attend school are filled with opportunity. Outstanding students who successfully complete the secondary school baccalaureate may receive scholarships or other types of financial support to attend university. But, Haiti's university system is still often unable to effectively serve all qualified secondary school students. So, some students will continue their education in other countries such as Dominican Republic, Canada, the United States or France. A great number of graduates, educated at Haitian universities at the expense of taxpayers, may also migrate to escape political turmoil, economic, and social problems. While students often migrate to other countries that will provide them with better employment opportunities, full-time and part-time faculty have also moved to other countries to seek better lives.

Rankit
Saint-Raphaël Municipality

Rankit, also known as Ranquitte, is in a rural central village in Haiti. The town is comprised of three districts: Bac-à-Soude, Cracaraille, and Bois-de-Lance. The quiet, beautiful, mountainous village has a population of approximately 20,000. The dirt, unpaved roads are travelled by the residents who get around town primarily on donkeys with a few motorcycles and very limited vehicles. Farming is the main economic reliance of people in the community. Farmers grow small crops of lemons, limes, pineapples, and oranges. However, Rankit is especially known for its coffee production, and coffee trees may be found on individual properties in the deep mountainous areas of the town. When Rankit was first colonized, it had a well-known reputation as a center of coffee production. Getting to the farms on the unpaved roads can be tedious, but the trek is not difficult for those who often walk the route from the lower lands to the hillside.

Some residing in the mountainous areas still do not have access to electricity, so hurricane lamps are commonly used in the remote location. After the 2010 earthquake ravaged

Port-au-Prince, many affected by the devastation returned to live in their native Rankit. They placed a burden on the already weak economy of this small town. For example, the added population affected enrollment of the barely-existent school system.

Rankit Secondary School

For many years, the closest public secondary school for students living in Rankit was not within walking distance. Furthermore, it was also not practical for students to go to the schools outside of Rankit because of limited transportation. But, even if students could walk, the roads between Rankit and other towns have been in such poor condition that it would be difficulty. The Rotary Partnership of Haiti saw the need for a secondary school and helped to make the residents' desire a reality. Children now have an opportunity to obtain an education at Rankit Secondary School, also known as Ranquitte Secondary School, the first public secondary school ever built in the town. On Friday, January 18th, 2013, the school was officially inaugurated. The Rotary Partnership of Haiti worked with Haiti Outreach for nearly two years to raise the funds to build the school. The seven classrooms, one for each secondary grade level, have the capacity for 60 students each. If the demand for the school exceeds that number, the administration is prepared to have two shifts. The school premises also include a large latrine, a well to access clean water, and a two-room administration building.

Boucan-Carré
Mirebalais District

Boucan-Carré is a town located in Haiti's Central Plateau region. The population was 56,028 on the 2015 census, and it continues to increase. While the surrounding area of the town was settled in the early 18th century, Boucan-Carré was not established until 1948 and was officially declared a municipality in April 1985. In the beginning, the town lacked adequate infrastructure. It did not have a hospital until recently when the clinic was upgraded. Also, the first primary and secondary schools were only built during the 21st century.

Residents in Boucan-Carré, who live below the poverty line, rely on raising livestock and selling it along with food and other commodities. However, Boucan-Carré is primarily a farming community, so the main activity is agriculture. Farmers grow a variety of crops such as corn, millet, sugar cane, pistachio, tobacco, pigeon peas, and beans, to name a few. Nevertheless, agriculture is not considered as profitable as it should be for farmers because they do not have technical training and support to implement up-to-date farming techniques.

The community has been plagued over the years by a number of issues. The excessive cutting of trees for charcoal has caused deforestations and erosion of the surrounding mountains. Another problem is that although some roads have been repaired, residents continue to contend with impassible roads in this remote area. Coupled with the ongoing road issues, residents in Boucan-Carré had to contend with an influx of people who were affected by the 2010 earthquake. This problem exacerbated the already poor living conditions that resulted in water contamination.

Lycée Dijon Jean Gilles of Boucan Carré

Boucan Carré, Lycée Dijon Jean Gilles of Boucan Carré is the only public secondary school in Boucan Carré and its rural surrounding areas. After opening, enrollment quickly increased from 250 to 300 students. The rented space was not sufficient to accommodate the additional students. So, a shift system was implemented which caused the overflow of students to be assigned to afternoon classes at the public primary school. The school is now housed in its own building, but it continues to be affected by problems. One such issue is that the school's population has been affected by insufficient and undrinkable water. Furthermore, sanitation continues to be a problem since the two cement latrines are not enough to accommodate the population that has increased to approximately 800 students. Such problems are also common at 90 percent of the primary schools located in Boucan Carré, and the neighboring institutions in other remote areas. Another problem for the school at the start was that teachers were not paid for some time until private funding was offered on a temporary basis. But a positive outcome for the school was that USAID funded a project for solar panels to be installed to provide basic lighting in classrooms.

La Victoire
Saint-Raphaël District

The city of La Victoire is located in the St. Raphael municipality of the North Department. The community, in the remote mountains, was founded in 1848 and officially established as a community in 1952. The population of the town was estimated as having 7,118 inhabitants in 1998. The number steadily increased to 8,011 in 2004 and has continued to rise since then. In spite of the consistent

increase of the population, health services are limited to a
center and a clinic. Furthermore, the community only
obtained its first secondary school in 2010. But, although
schools and medical facilities are now available to
residents, they still do not have access to other necessary
infrastructure as of this writing. Yet, these low-income
residents continue to manage. Farming is the main source
of income for the community. Farmers participated in a
project where they were assisted in growing peanuts. This
project enabled them to realize not only the nutritional
benefits that the crop would provide to them and their
families but also that the sale of the crop would be a vital
source of income.

La Victoire Public Secondary School

Children living in La Victoire have been attending one of
the three public primary schools over the years. But the
community did not have any public secondary school until
the 21st century. The Rotary Partnership of Haiti saw a dire
need for children in the community to receive secondary
education beyond 6th grade learning. After two years of
planning and establishing a formal relationship with Twin
Cities, a not-for-profit organization, and various fundraising activities, construction of the school began and was
completed for its inaugural on October 11, 2010. La
Victoire Public Secondary School serves up to 400
students. This school has allowed children to be able to
continue their education without having to travel long
distances or to live in a different community which was
costly for their parents. So, the opening of the school meant
that parents no longer had to incur significant extra
expenses which very few could even afford. Those students
now have an option to obtain secondary education without
having to end their schooling at an early age. The Haitian
Ministry of Education has taken over the responsibilities of

providing staff, support, and maintaining the school. In
addition to the classrooms, the school provides a library
which is equipped with computers that are powered by a
solar electrification system inside a lab.

Terrier-Rouge
North East Province

Terrier-Rouge is a community located in the north eastern
part of the country. The green hillside to the south greatly
contrasts the parched flat lands that stretch from Terrier-
Rouge to the ocean. Approximately 20,000 people reside in
Terrier-Rouge. It is estimated that 40 percent of the
population work as casual laborers because they do not
have permanent jobs. Those who have regular income work
primarily in areas such as mechanics, construction, and
agriculture. Agriculture, however, does not produce enough
to be a profitable business for many. Rearing livestock is
also a popular source of income along with selling the
livestock and other products at the local market.

Steady development is apparent throughout the town with
economic and financial infrastructures that include a hotel,
restaurants, bakeries, small grocery stores, banks, a funeral
home, and other businesses. However, the business
expansions have not extended to the construction of
satisfactory roads. The poor state of the roads has greatly
affected movements of residents and business ventures
around Terrier-Rouge. In spite of difficulties faced by the
residents, educational advancements are available for
students to attend any of the nine secondary schools and
continue to the agricultural vocational school.

Centre D'Agriculture St. Barnabas

Centre D'Agriculture St Barnabas is an agricultural school near Terrier-Rouge. The institution was initially created to provide further training to farmers who could not afford to go to school. The school, known for its organically grown crops, evolved into a two-year agriculture technical institution. It offers students courses in sustainable farming practices with an emphasis on water and soil conservation. The institution's vision is to provide viable agricultural services to Haiti's northern region.

Students not only gain agricultural skills but, as trained agricultural technicians, they are also able to share what they learn with farmers in their communities. Centre D'Agriculture St. Barnabas accepts applications from students around the country outside of it northern location. The training that students receive at the institution is considered equivalent to the teachings at a community college in the United States. Once students graduate, they are equipped to transition directly into agri-business and farming operations. They are also encouraged to consider entrepreneurship with financial aid available to open their own businesses.

Port-au-Prince
Western Province

Port-au-Prince became the capital of the newly independent Haiti in 1804. The capital also serves as the chief port and commercial center of the country. The population of the area is estimated at 1,230,000. The majority of the population is of African descent, but a prominent biracial minority controls many of the city's businesses. Unemployment in Port-au-Prince is high and compounded further by underemployment. But, the survival of Haitians is recognized by different aspects of economic activity throughout the city, especially among vendors selling goods and services. Also, other informal employment is prevalent in Port-au-Prince's slums, and this is essential for many to endure their difficult lives of poverty. High unemployment is determined as one reason for the steady rise of crime in the city center, but this issue is at a much lower rate in the upscale neighborhoods. Further social and financial setbacks occurred in January 2010 after a powerful earthquake, of magnitude 7.0. Thousands were killed or injured, and large areas of the city and surrounding towns were reduced to rubbles. Students were displaced when a number of school buildings were destroyed. But many of the buildings have since been repaired or rebuilt.

Canado Technique

Canado Technique opened in 1973. The technical school offers post-secondary educational programs. It is an option for secondary students who choose to pursue a technical course of education versus attending a university. The nationally known Canado Technique is considered a higher-level technical school. Potential students are expected to present a Philo certificate to confirm they passed the Philo exam that is taken prior to the national exam at the end of the final two years of secondary school

During the initial years of the school's opening, students enrolled in programs such as electricity, refrigeration, electronics, auto mechanics and diesel mechanics along with other vocational training courses. In 1990, to meet the demands of the labor market, computer networking and accounting courses were introduced. The school later expanded its two-year program to focus not only on telecommunications, industrial and electro-mechanics, but also on information technology and business subjects to address the needs of a growing student population for new training programs for employment.

Students may apply for scholarships from Haitian Scholarship, the Crosby Fund, and other organizations that provide funding towards the costs to finance their education. The school is also affiliated with the National Institute of Vocational Training (INFP) under the Ministry of National Education and Vocational Training. The Canadian government has continued to support the institution by paying faculty salaries and contributing towards the maintenance of the premises and equipment at the school.

University of Port-au-Prince

The University of Port-au-Prince (UP) is one of the many universities now open to students living in Port-au-Prince or elsewhere on the island. It is an option for students who may not have achieved the strict enrollment guidelines to enroll in the University of Haiti, or for those who cannot afford to pay the higher tuitions charged at popular private universities. UP, a public for-profit university, was initially known as the Institute of Management and Accounting. The school offered primarily business courses when it was founded in 1983. UP was the concept of a group of university professors and researchers who wanted to create a learning environment where they could share their knowledge, academic skills, and teaching methods with students.

The university has expanded throughout the years in response to the needs of the labor market and now includes the Faculty of Administrative Sciences, the Faculty of Legal Sciences, the Faculty of Economic Sciences, the

Faculty of Humanities and Letters, the Faculty of Arts, Computer Science and the Institute of Political Science. Students at UP are expected to develop into graduates who will promote the economic, political, cultural, and social development of Haiti. As such, the university's administrators are mindful of the need to participate in cultural activities that are focused particularly on strategies in sustaining the development of the population. Through those efforts, the university expects to incorporate the customary academic teachings with instructional approaches that promote Haitian cultural identity. This teaching technique is in contrast to former instructional practices where teachings were aligned with French language and culture rather than towards labor, community needs, Afro-Haitian history, and culture. The method of teaching at UP is intended to encourage students to identify and appreciate a need to give back to Haiti or their communities once they graduate.

Spanish Caribbean Territories and Education

Cuba, Puerto Rico, and the Dominican Republic are former colonies of Spain and located in the Caribbean. There were two periods of mass migration of slaves into these Spanish Caribbean territories. Before 1641, 240,000 Africans were transported to the colonies in the Caribbean and in Central America. The descendants of those slaves lost their African culture because they were forced to assimilate into the Hispanic mainstream. Those with white fathers could identify themselves as white or colored Creole. The second migration occurred when slaves were transported from other Caribbean territories to work in the Spanish colonized territories. They took their African customs with them and were less accepting in integrating into the dominant European culture. Some of those cultural habits still exist today since they have been passed down from generation to generation.

Throughout the three Spanish colonized islands in the Caribbean, the objective of the government was to integrate the Black ex-slave population into the school system that was developed by the white majority residents. Some Afro-Cuban societies opened their own schools during the 20th century so they could control their own teachings. However, for the most part, Afro-Latinos had no choice but to transitions into the public-school system and adhere to the policies that did not take their needs and culture into consideration. This meant that learning about the history and culture of Afro-Latinos was not incorporated into the curriculum. Instead, schools were uncompromising in working towards Europeanizing Afro-Latino students with teachings from a foreign curriculum. In such an educational system where whites could easily relate, they performed better than Afro-Latino students. So, they had more opportunities to transition to secondary schools and even universities that had been established as far back as the 16th century in Dominican Republic and 17th century in Cuba.

Cuba
Education During and After Slavery

Cuba was the last Caribbean territory to abolish slavery when Afro-Cubans were emancipated in 1886. Throughout the 18th century, learning was limited to private tutoring for wealthy white families while other white children attended church-based or secular schools that relied on fees or donations. Records indicate that people of African descent received some form of education during the early years of slavery. Twelve schools existed for them to attend by 1833 in contrast to 210 schools for white children. Students attending the 12 schools would quite possibly be biracial Cubans who were descendants of the first set of workers transported to the island during the 1600s. By 1842, the law required primary and secondary public schools to be built adjacent to each other within communities. Only white and free biracial children aged 7 to 10 were expected to attend those public schools. During the 1880s after the abolition of slavery, every community of more than 500 residents was mandated to establish one school for boys and one for girls with no racial divisions. The total number of schools increased steadily from 535 to 904 between 1883 and 1895 (Sierra, n.d.). However, Afro-Cubans were refused entry to many of these government-built schools. In fact, some public-school administrators also enforced a special fee to prevent impoverished Afro-Cubans from attending. This injustice caused some municipalities to operate separate schools for Afro-Cuban children. According to Sierra (n.d.), in 1883, Afro-Cubans living in Havana, led by Francisco Bonet and Antonio Rojas appealed to Governor General Emilio Calleja to allow their children to attend municipal-run schools all over the island. The Governor General's response emphasized that discrimination was unacceptable and un-Christian since it impacted the integration of people within Cuban society. The increase of Afro-Cuban children in public schools caused whites to open as many private schools as possible so their children would learn separately from Afro-Cubans.

In 1899, Afro-Cubans wanted education for their children that was equitable to the high standards of their white counterparts. Rafael Serra emphasized that the most important issue affecting the Afro-Cuban population was the lack of equal education, and an education was the only way to escape the inferiority status that prevented them from achieving racial equality (de la Fuente, 2001). Despite the requests, by the early to mid-20th century, some of the best religious schools in Cuba such as Ruston Academy, Candler College, La Progresiva, and Cathedral School were opened only to whites (de la Fuente, 2001). Even Spanish associated schools such as Colegio Champagnat and Colegio de Belen engaged in discriminatory practices. Catholic schools for girls such as the Buenavista Girls School was known to exclude Afro-Cubans up until the mid-1950s. The Havana Military Academy, which started in 1947, enrolled a few biracial students from wealthy families but did not enroll any Afro-Cubans to join its 500-student population. These private schools flourished because they were able to provide middle-class and wealthy whites with opportunities to segregate their children in an environment where Afro-Cubans were not allowed.

Afro-Cubans were dissatisfied with the discriminatory practices that prevented their enrolment in private schools. They knew that attending a private school could lead to opportunities for advancements in life. Yet, discriminatory practices prevented them from doing so. Attending public school gave them a feeling of being inferior to those attending prestigious private schools. These feelings caused a lower enrollment of Afro-Cuban children in public elementary schools than the enrollment of impoverished whites and biracial students.

When the communist regime, under the leadership of Fidel Castro, proposed laws to curtail injustices against the poor and Afro-Cubans by regulating private education, the suggestion was heavily supported by Afro-Cubans especially Club Atenas, the most exclusive of the Afro-Cuban societies during that period. The law was never approved by Congress, but it gained support and brought awareness of the discriminatory practices of private schools in Cuba.

Even in some professional schools, such as normal schools, the enrollment rate of Afro-Cubans was lower than other groups. For instance, only 10 percent of Afro-Cuban students enrolled in the Havana Normal School for female teachers when it opened. Furthermore, Afro-Cubans who enrolled in normal schools faced many prejudices. The communist leader Juan Marinello mentioned that students at the normal schools experienced a conspiracy that ensured Afro-Cubans were seen but not heard. They were barred from participating in social activities that demonstrated their visibility and representation in social events which included music bands (la Fuente, 2001). Opportunities were also not better for Afro-Cubans in higher education. As far back as 1929, some Afro-Cubans complained that they were given lower grades than whites. Also, at the private university, Universidad Catolica Santo Tomas de Villanueva, no Afro-Cubans were accepted. Furthermore, during the 1940s and early 1950s, Afro-Cubans represented only 15 - 20 percent of the 15,000-student body at the University of Havana.

Since 1961, the government took charge of the educational system in Cuba. One of its important actions was to nationalize private institutions at all levels of education. Another effort was to provide a 100 percent subsidized education system to enable all Cuban students, regardless of color or class, to attend all levels of school at no cost. So, with the Cuban revolution's outlaw of all forms of formal discrimination and institutional racism, many Afro-Cubans, who were the lowest on the social scale, benefited from the wide-reaching reforms that entitled them to obtain free education from pre-school to university. Despite the government's intentions that allowed Afro-Cubans to gain access to equitable education, institutional racism has continued. Even under the communist regime, the best schools still enroll primarily the children of the elite. (Leiner, 1985). According to Hawkins (2017), Miguel Martinez Malgares, an Afro-Cuban painter, wrote that if an Afro-Cuban wants to succeed in school, he or she must work twice as hard.

The U.S. State Department estimates that 62 percent of Cubans are of Black or mixed heritage. The largest combined number of residents with Afro-Cuban heritage live in the eastern region of Cuba in the adjacent provinces of Guantánamo, Santiago de Cuba, and Granma. During the 1800s, a great number of African slaves worked at the sugar mills throughout the eastern province. After the occupation of the Spanish ended in 1899, the eastern provinces became a refuge for Afro-Cubans who lived there from generation to generation. Although their lives were better in the east than anywhere else in Cuba, they still experienced problems, such as extensive poverty, because of continued oppression by wealthy Cuban landowners. For instance, land investments from foreign nationals, such as the United Fruit Company, displaced Afro-Cubans and exacerbated tensions when the company employed immigrant workers from Haiti and Jamaica. In response to this and tyrannical conditions, Afro-Cubans rebelled in the 1912 Race War. Their actions included burning down businesses and property owned by foreign investors. The Cuban government retaliated with the army who burned property of Afro-Cubans and massacred thousands of their own citizens in support of the foreign investors. Today, most of the descendants of slaves and immigrants from Haiti, Jamaica, and other Caribbean islands still reside in throughout the eastern region. They not only speak Spanish, but some Haitian communities exist where their creole language is still spoken. Communities may also be found in the eastern region where immigrants from English speaking Caribbean islands settled during the 1940s through the 1950s.

Santiago de Cuba
Santiago de Cuba Province

Santiago de Cuba Province is the second most important province in Cuba after the Havana Province. Located in the eastern part of Cuba, a distinct African culture is present in its namesake city with the largest number of descendants of African heritage in the country. During the 1800s, a significant number of African slaves were brought to Santiago de Cuba to work at the sugar mills. Other slaves, to a lesser extent, were transported from neighboring islands, primarily Haiti, because they were cheap and efficient laborers. In addition to sugar, the slaves worked coffee plantations in the highlands around Santiago de Cuba. More Haitians arrived in the city during the late 18th century after the Haitian Slave Revolt when they fled along the Windward Passage to eastern Cuba. That migration continued up until the 19th century. Since so many Afro-Cubans are descendants of Haitian immigrants, their Haitian heritage is depicted through their daily lives and participation in festivals.

Children to octogenarians celebrate carnival every July in
the capital city of Santiago de Cuba, also known as City of
Heroes. The diverse population do not expect to get much
sleep during the popular tradition. For an entire week, the
residents honor St. James the Apostle, the patron saint, with
music, dance, street food, processions, tractor-driven floats,
masquerades, effigies, and costume-clad revelers. Some of
the bands, known as carabali, trace their roots to the 19th
century with their costume designs going as far back as
slavery and colonialism Such festivities indicate how these
Afro-Cubans have preserved their heritage through
language, traditions, stories, and expressions which they
have passed down from one generation to the next.

July is also the time to celebrate Festival del Caribe, which
some call Festival of the Fire. For these five-day
celebrations, the population attend conferences, panel
discussions, and lectures on the cultural aspects of Santiago
de Cuba. Moreover, participants visiting from neighboring
Caribbean nations allow Afro-Cubans to maintain
knowledge of their heritage and practices. In addition, there
are performances, exhibitions, and folklore renditions
throughout the city. The festival culminates with a street
parade and the burning of a papier-mache effigy which is
followed by merriment in the streets. Residents of Santiago
de Cuba may obtain history and heritage information too at
the Fernando Ortiz African Cultural Center.

Secundaria Basica Jose Antonio Echeverria Bianchi

Secundaria Basica Jose Antonio Echeverria Bianchi was
founded in 1963 in Santiago de Cuba after the revolution.
The institution was built to address the population's long-
standing expectations that students who completed primary
school at the grade 6 would have an opportunity to continue
their education instead of leaving school at such an early

age. The school has an enrollment of approximately 350 students and 30 teachers. Similar to other secondary schools, this institution caters to children between the ages of 12 to 14 years old. When students complete primary school, they enter this institution at grade 7 and leave at grade 9. Throughout those grades, students learn basic subjects so they will progress to either upper pre-university education or technical studies professional education. The institution's sports' curriculum distinguishes it from other secondary schools because the specialty program brings together students with sports talents. The sports courses enable students to engage not only in working on their athletics skills but learn about the academic side for at least 16 disciplines in sports.

Boys wear the mustard colored pants and girls wear the mustard colored skirts which is the standard uniform of all students who attend basic secondary schools throughout Cuba. In continuing with the political indoctrination from elementary school, the main objectives of this school is also to ensure that students demonstrate patriotism, reject capitalism, and become consciously familiar with the Cuban socialist expectations - to love and respect the heroes and other ideals.

Escuela Camilo Cienfuegos

Escuela Camilo Cienfuegos is one of a number of military schools in Cuba that was first opened in 1966, after the revolution, to educate children of martyrs and fighters of the rebel army. Initially, boys and young men received primary and secondary education at the school. By 1977, the school in Santiago de Cuba was expanded to provide pre-university curriculum. The mission has remained throughout the years to educate young people who want to pursue a military career. But those potential candidates must go through a selective admissions' process. Enrollment expectations require students to possess certain qualities such as reasonable physical and mental abilities, high political values, exceptional moral and disciplinary standards, and the continued commitment to train as officers for the Revolutionary Armed Forces. Once admitted, students select specialty areas of study and maintain studies of those subjects while they progress through different class levels. The military school's curriculum correlates with the Ministry of Education's higher secondary education standards and covers the specific and vocational interests of military life appropriately. In addition to classroom learning, all-round student experiences include participation in patriotic and military activities. Graduates at Escuela Camilo Cienfuegos can continue their studies at higher education institutions.

Professional School of Music Esteban Salas

Professional School of Music "Esteban Salas" is a well-known music school that was founded in 1959 in Santiago de Cuba. It opened its doors to students in 1960. Students from the eastern and central parts of Cuba received practical instructions in playing instruments such as the piano, violin, viola, violoncello and guitar. Once the students progressed to the middle level, they were expected to display their musical talents by playing as a group at public venues. Professional School of Music "Esteban Salas" became associated with the Provincial Art School from 1967. This connection meant that, in addition to the practical teaching of instruments, students could now receive musical theory instructions that had existed at Provincial Art School. In 1986, the conservatory changed its name to the Provincial School of Music "Esteban Salas" and later adopted its current name, Professional School of Music "Esteban Salas".

The school encourages graduates to work with students or form their own bands to continue developing their musical talents. Some of these conservatory groups include a chamber orchestra, female choir, and a combined choir. Graduates are expected to apply what they have learned to preserve Cuban music and its cultural heritage. These graduates also participate in competitions and festivals organized by the conservatory throughout provinces.

Facultad de Ciencias Médicas # 1

For many years, medical institutions were non-existent in the province of Santiago de Cuba. So, pre-university graduates interested in continuing their studies in the medical area had to relocate to other provinces. On February 10th, 1962, the School of Medicine of the Universidad de Oriente was opened in that neglected province. Three years later, the institution was relocated and officially opened as a medical school on October 19th, 1964. During the earlier years, only those students specializing in medicine were accepted. But the school later expanded its offerings to students seeking bachelor's degrees in nursing or health technology. Additions to course offerings were made by the 2001 - 2002 academic year with the bachelor's degree in psychology. The institution is accredited by the National Accreditation Board. Students enrolled in post-graduate studies may choose from at least one of 24 medical specialties.

Universidad de Oriente

The Universidad de Oriente was founded in October of 1947. This was a period when secondary education for people of African descent was a low priority for the government, so these residents were not expected to gain acceptance to Universidad de Oriente. However, today, students of African descent in the province have a chance to attend the university which is considered the second major center of higher education in Cuba and the first of the eastern region. The initial enrollment was 170 students with 30 professors. At that time, students completed courses offered in the faculty of their choice such as engineering, philosophy, education, law, and commercial sciences. In 1953, the first graduation occurred with 67 students. By 1954, the increased enrollment required an expansion to a two-story building. During the Revolution in the 1950s, the university was closed temporarily. Some professors migrated in their opposition to the communist government. Since the re-opening, the university restructured its offerings and added a number of new programs. The continued increase in enrollment caused a need in 1976 new buildings and to also add academic programs. By 2002, campuses were opened in all the municipalities of the province of Santiago de Cuba.

Guantánamo
Guantánamo Province

Guantánamo is the most eastern province in Cuba. The province is home to the largest number of people of African heritage in the country. The arrival of slaves began with the transport of Africans to work on sugar plantations throughout the Guantánamo Province. The population increased during the Haitian revolution when many French landowners left with their slaves and settled in Guantánamo Province to re-establish their former sugar and coffee plantations. Another influx of people of African descent occurred when Jamaicans and other West Indians migrated to work on sugar plantations but later used their fluent English to obtain better-paying jobs at the U.S. naval station.

The Cuban revolution in 1959 ended mass migration from neighboring islands. Nevertheless, the descendants of African slaves and migrants have continued to maintain the vibrant celebrations of their ancestors who kept festivals in huts on the sugar cane or coffee plantations (Bauza, 2002). In La Loma del Chivo community, residents dance in the streets to the sounds of bongo and marimbula as they revel at the ending of the five-day Festival of Changüí. The festival began during the 19th century as a dedication to African slaves.

Afro-Cubans of Haitian descent have also passed down their traditions such as Tumba Francesa, a unique form of Haitian-style music and dance that community groups continue to perform. These performers dance to the rhythm of African drums just as their ancestors moved to dances that mimicked the French minuet and quadrille. In fact, Tumba Francesa was designated as one of the Intangible Cultural Heritage of Humanity by UNESCO in 2003. Haitian descendants in Guantánamo have also continued the tradition of communicating in Haitian Creole.

Afro-Cubans of British West Indian descent have maintained their traditions in their English-speaking community. They still cook the customary Jamaican dishes such as saltfish and dumplings or prepare Jamaica's national dish - ackee. The British West Indian Welfare Centre, founded in 1945, served as an English language school and a center for thousands of newly arriving immigrants from the islands (Bauza, 2002). It was a place where immigrants could get away from the injustices experienced by Afro-Cubans and immigrants prior to the Revolution. Today, the center provides the community with archival and current information. It also remains open for members to conduct regular meetings, talk about sports such as cricket, hold book club readings, have dinners, teach English classes, and engage in educational workshops. Work at the center continues towards preserving all aspects of the British West Indian culture so upcoming generations will maintain traditions.

IPVCE José Maceo Grajales

The Pre-university Vocational Institute of Exact Sciences (IPVCE) "José Maceo Grajales" was founded in October 1981, more than 20 years after the Revolution. Approximately 3,000 students are enrolled at the largest educational complex in the Guantánamo Province. This secondary school system for outstanding students was long-awaited for the province with the largest population of residents of African heritage. So, children finally had an opportunity to attend a pre-university school. The competitive entrance requirements have meant that only those with the best grades are selected to attend the school where science and technology are the focus. Throughout the three years of attendance, students must maintain exceptional grades to continue their studies until graduation in grade 12. The school has a 98 percent high rate of excellence in its graduation of students who progress to one of the universities to continue their studies in areas such as medicine, dentistry, engineering and other careers. In addition to demonstrating high achievements on the national examination finals, students at IPVCE José Maceo Grajales have been awarded first place in national and international competitions in biology, spelling, computer, and other academic areas. In fact, the Ministry of Education recognized the school's many accomplishments when the ministry held the 16th National Spelling Contest on the campus of IPVCE José Maceo Grajales instead of its usual practice of holding the competition at a school in Havana. Despite the rigorous curriculum, students have also become involved in activism which included their vocal demonstration that the United States have imposed an economic, commercial, and financial blockade against Cuba.

Bayamo
Granma Province

Granma Province is located on the western side of Santiago de Cuba. It does not have a large population of Afro-Cubans in comparison to the Santiago de Cuba and Guantánamo provinces, but the sizable population in Granma Province surpasses Afro-Cubans in other provinces throughout the island. Bello & Aliaga (2017) report that in 1781 to 1800, many slaves were transported from Jamaica to Bayamo, Granma's capital city. Bayamo was a valuable hub during the Spanish slave trade especially because sugarcane crops became the predominant economic asset of the area. As a result, Jamaican slaves combined their heritage with the Cuban culture to form a strong cultural base in the area. Today, Afro-Cubans represent the second largest population in the Granma Province. They continue to be outnumbered by the bi-racial population who, for the most part, will not admit to their African roots.

Slaves in Bayamo lived an uncustomary life as compared to those elsewhere in Cuba and other colonies of Spain. Throughout the countryside of the province, slaves were not only employed as laborers, but they held positions as administrators of farms where they enjoyed relative independence. In fact, some slaves became property owners and often engaged in commercial transactions by using licenses attached to their owners' cattle, houses, and other properties (Bello & Aliaga, 2017). Such relaxed way of life made it easier for them to save money with the intentions of purchasing their freedom or the liberty of their family. Bello & Aliaga (2017) also reports that verification would confirm some slaves could afford to lend money not only to other slaves but even to their own masters. Another uncommon experience for slaves was that the laws in Granma Province supported their right to make requests to be purchased by a new master. This became a common practice that was frowned upon by owners.

At the Granma Province's annual festival, people of African descent may show off their heritage by displaying culinary skills, music, dance, and other aspects of their culture passed down to them. Another highlight of Granma Province is La Demajagua Sugar Estate. It is popularly known as the place where slaves were the first ones in Cuba to obtain freedom at the start of the liberation war with Spain. While the heroics of the estate's owner have always been recognized in writings, this former sugar plantation will remain symbolic of the many slaves who toiled the soil and did other back-breaking work under in-humane conditions. A collection of testimonial objects that preserve those memories of the slaves' experiences are housed at La Museo Historico Demajagua on the estate. They include shackles and chains to fasten slaves and also the artistic pottery work of slaves.

Escuela Tecnica General Milanes

Escuela Tecnica General Milanes was founded in 1945. The school opened its doors in Bayamo in a small room two years later. The opening finally gave the majority population of Afro-Cubans and biracial residents a chance to take community-related classes in dairy farming, general mechanics, woodworking, food industry, internal combustion machines, plumbing, masonry, welding, and dress-making. At the end of 1953, the growth of the institution, to as many as 100 students, required a move to larger facilities with better conditions. A new building with more spacious classrooms and offices were constructed with overwhelming support from all stakeholders in the community and the Ministry of Education. The bank made donations of essential tools and equipment for students to use in workshops. Support, however, did not extend to the school's electrical expenses which had to be paid by teachers. By the end of the 1949 – 1950 school year, only 37 students graduated while the others dropped out. Due to declining resources, the drop-out rate increased even further by the 1952 - 1953 school year when only five students graduated.

Throughout the years, student enrollment and retention, classroom facilities, in addition to equipment and tools have improved. Furthermore, students have more selections that include classes in physics, chemistry, radio mechanics, electricity, cosmetology, and other subjects. For the 2017 - 2018 school year, approximately 2,450 students were enrolled in 36 specialties. Learning is also geared towards the outside community. Workshops are conducted for outside entities to enhance workforce skills. The school's community involvement was rewarded when it received the National Educational Tradition Award from the Association of Pedagogues of Cuba (APC) for its outstanding work in training qualified workers and mid-level technicians throughout the decades. Community involvement also includes partnering with local organizations and companies such as the Raw Material Recovery Company.

Dutch Caribbean Territories
and Education

The Dutch was involved in the Transatlantic Slave Trade from 1596 to 1829. Dutch traders brought 400,000 slaves to Suriname; 100,000 to the Spanish colonies via Curacao; 25,000 to Recife; 16,000 to Essequibo; 15,000 to Berbice; and 11,000 to Demerary (Steljn, 2013). The Dutch colonies eventually became known as Suriname, Curacao, Saba, St. Eustatius, St. Martin, Aruba, and Bonaire. African slaves settled and worked primarily on sugar plantations (The Colonial Williamsburg Foundation, n.d.). By the 18th century, nearly one-in-ten enslaved people in Suriname escaped from their brutal working conditions, and they established or joined Maroon communities located throughout rural, mountainous areas far out of the reach of their slave masters. The Netherlands was one of the last occupiers to abolish slavery in 1863.

During slavery, the ruling class did not permit the enslaved or other non-Dutch to learn their native Dutch language. Unlike the British and other colonizers, the Dutch did not try to convert their slaves to Christianity because such action would require teaching their language to slaves which would have resulted in slaves becoming literate. Due to the restrictions in learning Dutch, slaves created their own way of communicating among themselves by combining different languages and other creative words which ultimately led to the Creole language of Papiamentu, a common form of communication today for the locals in Aruba, Bonaire, and Curacao - the ABC islands.

The education system of the former Netherlands Antilles originated primarily from the Dutch system. Education is compulsory from four years old to 18 years old. Students have the option of attending private schools which are mainly Catholic or public schools that are funded by the government. In the schools, students are taught in Papiamento or Dutch or English. For instance, in primary schools, Papiamento and Dutch are taught in Bonaire while English and Dutch are the languages of instruction at schools in St. Eustatius and Saba. However, in secondary schools, Dutch is the language of instruction and examination in Bonaire and St Eustatius while Papiamento is an elective in Bonaire schools.

Suriname
Education During and After Slavery

Prior to the mid-18th century, education in Suriname was provided for whites only. Slaves were kept illiterate from even receiving baptismal or religious education because whites had the common notion that an educated slave would be dangerous. On the other hand, some plantation owners allowed their biracial children to obtain an education by sending them to the best schools in Suriname and even sometimes to Europe. Such schooling gave this group the social-economic benefits of uplifting their status to prominent positions that were previously dominated by the minority white ruling class. As such, they became a powerful sub-elite group (Randeraad, 1998). Also, church and state instigated the opening of a private school in 1760 for those free biracial children whose parents could afford to pay the nominal fees. Later during the 19th century, public schools or "town schools" were opened for free biracial children who came from poor backgrounds and could not afford to attend a private school.

During the 1840s, planters realized that emancipation would be inevitable because the adjacent colonies, British Guyana and French Guiana, already emancipated their slaves. As a result, planters allowed the Moravian church to begin christening and educating slaves under the premise that the teachings would make them civilized so that they could become disciplined members of the society (Randeraad, 1998). The Emancipation Act, Article 25, supported the education of ex-slaves because its contents included that the colonial government must provide them with religious and academic education.

Slavery was abolished in Suriname in 1863, but workers were not fully emancipated until after apprenticeship.

During the time of full emancipation in the 1870s, the local government opened primary schools in Paramaribo and other known towns without authorization from the Minister of Colonies in Netherland (Thomas, 2014). In response, the minister who controlled the education budget steadily decreased funding to Suriname. Furthermore, when the first government secondary school opened in 1887 in Paramaribo, the minister retaliated against the disregard of his authority by closing the school three months after the founding. The minister also believed that higher education was not necessary for the majority population – primary school was sufficient. Subsequently, he agreed to extend the final primary school level for those who wanted to continue their schooling. But, this basic education for the Afro-Surinamese did not provide them with the opportunities for upward mobility. In fact, they realized that free education was a method for the colonial state to keep control of them. The control tactics extended more so to the rural agricultural districts with less attention from the government to open primary schools. This injustice supported the insecurities of planters that highly educated students would no longer want to work on their plantations or would start their own farms in competition against the planters.

Protestant missionaries opened schools in some rural villages occupied by runaway slaves and their descendants during the 18th century. State elementary schools were eventually opened in many rural villages as late as the 1960s. The disparities in education has been evident in remote villages throughout the Rainforest. According to Thomas (2014) the quality of education in Paramaribo is different from the teachings in deep rural Maroon communities where imparting the basics was sufficient for students to seek employment as laborers on agricultural estates. The basic teachings included limited Dutch language, reading, writing and arithmetic in deteriorating facilities with poorly trained and paid teachers.

Even today, some students who live in remote Maroon villages must end their education after completing primary school since no secondary school is located in their community or nearby. In other rural communities where a rare junior secondary school is located, Maroons and indigenous children could pass the grade 6 entrance exam, but they may have to contend with issues that will prevent them from attending (Kambel & MacKay 1999). Some problems include: the unaffordable costs for boarding in another city or town if they live far away from the school; school fees are expensive; the quality of instruction does not take cultural familiarity into consideration; unqualified teachers at understaffed schools; switching from native language at home to instruction and textbooks in Dutch; inadequate toilet facilities, running water, and/or electricity. Despite these obstacles, a growing number of parents will do all that is possible for their child to attend a senior secondary school and post-secondary schools in other districts or Paramaribo. The number of students living in rural villages who attend secondary schools and the university is increasing annually (Committee on the Elimination of Racial Discrimination, 2013).

Pokigron and Atjoni
Sipaliwini District

Pokigron is a remote rural village in the interior of Suriname. It is recognized for a number of reasons. First, it is the last village in the Sipaliwini District that is accessible by road from Paramaribo, which is approximately 115 miles away or a three to four-hour bus drive. So, the town serves as the starting point to travel to the other villages along the Upper-Suriname River by motorized dug-out canoes. Atjoni is the harbor community adjacent to Pokigron that was established to transport goods and people to the Rainforest communities located around the Upper Suriname River. It is also considered a communications and service hub for all the other villages that are accessible only by boat. Between Pokigron and the Atjoni harbor community, there are approximately 400 homes. Both communities share a primary school, a secondary school, a clinic, and several supermarkets with the remote communities located throughout the rainforest along the Upper Suriname River

Although Pokigron is described as a quiet, sleepy village, it is home to the oldest and one of the largest Maroon indigenous groups in Suriname, the Saramaccans. The ancestors of the Saramaka or Saramacca were among those Africans sold as slaves to Europeans in Suriname during the late 17th and early 18th centuries. They worked the region's sugar, timber, and coffee plantations. In 1690, the first mass escape of slaves occurred, and they became the core of a Maroon community. Those who escaped to the rainforest prior to emancipation were feared, and they fought tirelessly for approximately 10 years to gain their independence. In 1712, the last significant influx of slaves escaped to the Maroon community (Darko Ankrah, 2013). According to Darko Ankrah (2013), by 1770, Maroons signed treaties with the Dutch, and the agreement not only ended the fighting but also the acceptance of other escaped slaves into the Maroon community. The Maroons were initially called Bush Negroes before they adapted the name Saramaka. The Saramaka remains the world's largest surviving population of Maroons.

VOJ-Atjoni Secondary School

For approximately 150 years after the abolition of slavery, children of Maroon decent living in Pokigron and Antjoni did not have access to a secondary school in the community until 2012 when VOJ – Atjoni, a junior-secondary school, was opened. It has served as an essential link in education for children residing not only in the Pokigron and Antjoni villages but also the surrounding communities where students must commute by boat. The junior secondary school started with two first year classes. Another first year class was added to accommodate additional students who passed the Grade 6 secondary school entrance exam. Thirty percent of these students of Maroon descent will excel academically to qualify for entrance to the general track of junior secondary school in comparison to approximately 50 percent of students living in cities such as Paramaribo (Stateuniversity.com, n.d.). In 2017, the school produced its first graduate from the Institute of Natural Resources and Engineering Studies, a post-secondary polytechnic institute where students focus on science and technology courses. This graduate now serves as a role model to students at VOJ-Atjoni who recognize that they too can achieve such academic success.

From time to time difficulties, common to most deep rural schools, have affected VOJ – Atjoni. For instance, an increase in the student population was expected for the 2017 school year so construction of four new classrooms began ahead of time. However, the work was not completed in time for the opening of school since the government failed to pay the contractors. As a result, 50 to 60 students who passed the Grade 6 entrance exam were turned away from entering VOJ - Atjoni. The suggested solution from the Ministry of Education, Science, and Culture was for those students to seek entrance instead at a junior secondary school located in Paramaribo. Of course, this option was not possible for families who could not afford for their children to reside in the city. Many said that the option was not acceptable for those students who worked so hard to pass the grade 6 entrance exam. Students, teachers, and parents demonstrated to voice their dissatisfactions. Another problem that faced VOJ-Atjoni during the same school period was the boarding school did not re-open for its 50 residents since the kitchen staff, cleaners, and gardeners stopped working to protest seven months of unpaid wages. A third issue is the discovery at one of the Children's Book Festival that children at VOJ – Atjoni and elsewhere in the community were not adequately learning the Dutch language to meet academic requirements. Last, the unpopularity in teaching at rural schools has impacted VOJ Atjoni over the years. The school has struggled with a shortage of teachers. At one point, eight teachers, the director, and vice president left the school within a short period of time while the remaining six teachers asked for transfers.

Moengo
Marowijne District

The Maroon village of Moengo, in the Ndyuka territory of the Cottica River basin, became known as the birthplace and primary location of Suriname's bauxite mining industry when Alcoa/Suralco began operations in 1916. By 1922 the mines began exporting ore from Moengo (Alcoa 2013). The demand for aluminum reached historic heights in 1943 because of its importance to militaries worldwide. This necessity caused Suriname to supply bauxite for three-quarters of North America's war needs. World War II caused further demand for Surinamese bauxite and by 1950, Suriname became Alcoa's primary source of bauxite (Connell, 2017).

In the beginning, Ndyuka Maroons were limited to cutting weeds and brush for Alcoa. But during later years, they were more valued because of their familiarity with the remote areas of the rainforest. The Maroon's knowledge helped Alcoa to learn about the land so the company could locate terrain that otherwise its personnel would not have been able to identify on their maps. In addition, Ndyuka Maroons were hired in 1922 to cut wood that was used to build the railway tracks, and in the process, they cleared the jungle's undergrowth for the railway.

During earlier years, the Surinamese government denied the Ndyuka Maroons from obtaining secondary education. Between the 1940s and 1970s, the government continued to prevent the Maroons from obtaining secondary education and other opportunities to achieve social advancements. So, the Maroons relied on working in permanent positions at Alcoa where they received inexpensive housing with free water and electricity, advanced sanitation, medical infrastructure, and loans to build their own houses. Moreover, the Ndyuka Maroons had access to a company store along with dairy and vegetable farms. So, despite the lack of secondary schooling, employment at Alcoa provided the Moengo Maroons with social development that ultimately benefitted their community.

Although certain employment offerings made a difference in the lives of those Ndyuka Maroons who worked for Alcoa, they were concerned about certain company practices. Connell (2017) reports that the mining company instituted a segregated community that depicted Suriname's ethnic, class, and gender hierarchies. Natives resided in cramped family houses and barracks while expatriates lived in a spacious, well-kept neighborhood with large houses, wide roads, and a social club for a variety of activities. The

Maroons were also affected by wage constraints as a result of racial hierarchy. Also, Alcoa's ban on unauthorized outside visitors meant that the Maroons lived in an isolated community. They were further cut-off from the rest of Suriname when a decision was made to increase mining productivity by turning back the clock one hour as opposed to the standard time adhered to throughout the rest of the country. Despite the presence Alcoa brought to Moengo, that town, without a main road, remained ever more separated from the rest of Suriname for many years. Moengo was accessible only by river until 1955 when an airstrip was built, and in 1964, a main road was constructed. But, a major concern of the Ndyuka Maroons was that they disapproved of Alcoa's extensive mining of the land. They considered the harsh mining practices for natural resources as destruction of their ancestral lands.

The employment of Maroons was impacted when all bauxite operations were suspended in 2015 by Alcoa after claiming their reserves were dwindling. In 2017, Alcoa announced that it would close the bauxite plant and leave the country. This was devastating news to the population in nearby Moengo that had relied and even flourished from Alcoa's presence apart from the six years setback from the civil war. Moengo changed from a once bustling town to a run-down community with crumbling infrastructure. Locals have said mining was replaced by a hustle culture in which people scrape out a living day-by-day. Nevertheless, places such as Tembe Art Studio, located in a wing of a shuttered hospital that Alcoa built, has made the town into an art center. The work of international artists adorns the town. In addition to getting permission from Alcoa to use the space, Alcoa's subsidiary donated $50,000 to fund a music/art studio. The studio promotes The Moengo Festival of Threatre and Dance and also art festivals where hosted artists-in-residence teach well-attended youth workshops.

Barronschool

Barronschool in Moengo, is a secondary school that provides vocational and technical education. The teaching staff of 27 serves approximately 500 students in the Ndyuka Maroon community. In addition to vocational and technical studies, the professional designated school offers practical courses. Students enrolled in the first and second years of the primary vocational education track are taught basic classes. During the third year, students are assigned to a track associated with their best subject performance. As such, they may be placed in a vocational practical track to focus on courses such as cooking, nutrition, or office practice. Another option after completing the second year is to place students in the lower technical school track. Here, students receive basic training in different technical courses such as building and construction. These courses serve as a lower level alternative to the advanced instructions that are offered to students attending senior secondary technical/vocational schools or junior secondary general education schools in Paramaribo. During the third and fourth year, students gain practical experience so that they will acquire skills to begin working when they graduate with a diploma. The school also offers an elementary vocational education track for those students who require remedial assistance in courses such as language, arithmetic, and other related subjects. This special program allows students to also obtain instruction in practical courses so they will learn a skill in the three-year certificate program.

Barronschool along with the primary schools were greatly impacted by the civil war from 1986 - 1992. So, the Ndyuka Maroon children were deprived of an education for some years since combat in the town destroyed the already poorly maintained government buildings. Once again, the community was deprived of schools that were long-awaited for centuries. Fortunately, the school obtained support from the Netherlands and other NGOs in the planning and construction of new buildings. University students attending an architectural and construction school in the Netherlands took on the challenge of rebuilding the school with guidance from their professors and other stakeholders outside and within the Ndyuka Maroon community. The need for labor to reconstruct the buildings led to the realization that although approximately 100 students in the construction program were enthusiastic to participate in the school's rebuilding, they could not do so because they were not taught the expected building skills (Koops, Oosterlaken, et. al. 2015). The discovery uncovered that immediate changes needed to be made to employ qualified construction teachers to provide adequate practical training to students. Nevertheless, teachers and students were passionate and productive in helping in any way they could with the renovation of classrooms, a library, a design classroom, three workshops and a computer laboratory with internet connected computers. The student population increased after renovation to approximately 600, and they have occupied 17 restored classrooms and five practical rooms. Students from the Netherland also constructed a greenhouse on the school's premises for agricultural projects. Throughout the years, the same university in the Netherlands has continued to provide their students to support to Barronschool's construction needs.

Albina
Marowijne District
and
Brokopondo
Brokopondo District

Albina is the capital of the Marowijne District that is located at the eastern border of French Guiana. Albina was founded around 1846 and became well-known to outsiders 30 years later when gold was discovered. During the early 20th century, Albina was no longer an isolated community since roads were built to enable easier travel from this remote village to Moengo where the bauxite plant was located. Major traffic to the village caused the need for development. A new hospital was built in Albina, and it also served as the local hospital for the entire Maroqijne District. In addition to the existing primary schools in Albina, the first secondary school was opened many years later. Prior to the civil war, 2,000 Maroon residents of Albina had access to all the amenities such as water supply, electricity, telephone, postal service, police, and customs services. Massive development and beautiful beaches attracted so many tourists to Albina that it was necessary to construct more hotel resorts and stores to meet the demands of guests. Additional visitors passed through Albina with the opening of the ferry connection from the city to St. Laurent du Maroni, French Guiana. However, the prosperity and the beautiful surroundings of Albina were greatly impacted during its 140 years of existence by the civil war in 1986 between the Maroons and government troops. Most of the residents in Albina and adjacent communities sought safety by fleeing to French Guiana to escape troops who resorted to slaughtering residents and burning down their houses and other buildings such as churches and schools. The district's administration moved while government offices and schools closed. Water and electricity were shut off. The previously well-maintained roads were destroyed, so Albina, once again, was cut off from the rest of Suriname. Since the end of the war, Netherlands and NGOs have aided in rebuilding Albina into the place it was before the war.

Brokopondo is the capital town of the Brokopondo District, its namesake. It is the third largest city in Suriname with an estimated population of 17,000. The town includes predominantly Saramaccan Maroons whose ancestry dates back to African runaway slaves. While African slaves could not obtain an education freely in Brokopondo, today schools are open to their descendants residing in the village and other nearby communities. The boat journey for those students from their villages to Brokopondo raises safety concerns since the boats do not have life jackets. Another issue for students attending school in Brokopondo is that parents often cannot afford to send them to school, so they frequently drop out before the age of 16 years.

Bokopondo is one of the few interior locations with a main road. This road has given residents a shorter and less stressful journey to Paramaribo. The road has made it possible for locals and residents to travel to and from the gold mines nearby the town. Access to information from the town has also become easier for Maroon residents since the construction of the main road.

The Brokopondo Reservoir, one of the world's largest reservoirs, is also located in the town. The reservoir is a major electricity producer, and it serves as an irrigation source during drought periods. Other infrastructures in the Brokopondo include a health center that serves not only residents in the town but also those in neighboring communities. In addition to the health center, the town is known for its rainforest attractions such as the Brownsberg

Nature Park where Leo Falls, different species of monkeys, and other rare animal breeds are located

Nucleus Teaching Centers

Two Nucleus Teaching Centers were established in collaboration with the Ministry of Regional Development and other ministries to serve schools in the Maroon towns of Brokopondo, Brokopondo District and Albina, Marowijne District. Prior to these rare teacher training centers, all training took place at teachers' colleges which are all located in Paramaribo. The Ministry of Education's aim in establishing both centers is to regionalize part of its services so that teachers in the interior regions may readily have access to resources and workshops in their communities without travelling long distance to Paramaribo. Furthermore, the centers were established to improve standards in remote village schools where educational achievements fall below schools located in Paramaribo.

Both Nucleus Centers are housed in modern facilities with classrooms containing supportive learning resources, a training room, meeting rooms, a library, a computer room and office space. Teachers obtain knowledge through formal and informal educational training in their subject areas. Also, the aim of the centers is to accommodate and strengthen local community development.

Flemish Association for Development Cooperation and Technical Assistance, a non-profit organization, has been responsible for implementing the training programs. In recognizing teacher training needs in Suriname's remote districts, the organization set a goal to attract and train as many teachers as possible. Initially, the organization had to deal not only with the challenges of having teachers seconded for training from schools where they were needed due to a teacher shortage, but the organization also had to contend that they were not trained as teacher trainers. Inoperable computers were another issue that affected training. Nevertheless, the organization has continued to provide resources that guide rural teachers in performance of their instructional duties despite difficulties in reaching so many teachers who are stretched throughout the vast remote rainforest. They are aware that the more training rural teachers receive, the better they will become in uplifting the learning abilities of Maroon children.

Nieu-Nickerie
Nickerie District

Nickerie is a district in the northwest section of Suriname and close to border of Guyana. The capital of the district, Nieuw-Nickerie, is the second largest town in Suriname. This is a farming community with rice and bananas as the most important crops. But farmers also grow cocoa, baboen lumber, and balata used in making golf balls for export. Slaves labored in the Nickerie District since 1797 when the first plantations were established in that area. Slaves also worked the thriving cotton and coffee plantations under British rule between 1804 and 1816.

The Afro-Surinamese living in Nickerie District make up the second largest cultural group. They maintain their cultural identity by participating in annual celebrations such as Keti Koti which marks Emancipation Day in Suriname when slavery was abolished in 1863. Another significant cultural reminder is the statue of the female slave Alida that was erected in Wageningen, a town located in the Nickerie District. The statue commemorates the atrocities of slavery and the colonial slave revolts against the European plantocracy in the once popular rice producing area. The legend of Alida is that her mistress, the cruel Susanna du Plessis, hacked off her left breast and served it to du Plessis's husband as punishment because he was attracted to Alida's voluptuous body. The statue was erected in 1973 to celebrate 110 years that slavery was abolished in Suriname. In addition, some residents in Nickerie District participate in Winti, another cultural tradition that dates back to African ancestry. Winti is a ritual prayer ceremony accompanied by drums. Participants go into a trance and perform supernatural acts that include dancing barefoot on broken glass or on hot coals and eating glass or other dangerous objects without any physical damage or cuts to the skin. Participants also cover part of their bodies with a white clay powder which they believe will bring them closer to the god.

Elsje Finck – Sanichar College COVAB

Elsje Fink-Sanichar College Central Training (EFS College) for nurses and practitioners of related professions was founded in 1982 with its main campus in Paramaribo. One of the institution's philosophies at its inception was to centralize nursing education. So, in 2011, the Nickerie campus was opened. Decentralization of the school was eminent to accommodate students who had to travel long distances from Nieu-Nickerie and surrounding villages to Paramaribo.

The Nickerie program started with 25 students for basic nursing training. These students came from the Nickerie Regional Hospital, the Regional Health Service, and Suriname Psychiatric Center. The college did not have suitable class accommodations in Nieu-Nickerie, so two classrooms and an office space were rented for theory instruction. For practical lessons, an equipped room was rented elsewhere. The first graduating class included 21 successful students out of the 25 students who initially enrolled. The graduating class included five men and 16 women nurses. This was a historic first in training residents in the Nickerie District to work as nurses in their communities. Since that first incoming class, student enrollment at the nursing school has grown rapidly. As a result, more spacious accommodations were found which includes two classrooms, one practical room, and one office space. Furthermore, the central location is within walking distance to the public transportation.

Paramaribo
Paramaribo District

Paramaribo is the capital and largest port of Suriname. The population of the city was greatly increased in 1873, 10 years after emancipation, when former slaves completed apprenticeship and were allowed to leave the sugar plantations. Their arrival in the city made it a predominantly Afro-Surinamese city. Now, 27 percent of the population are bi-racial residents of African descent. Approximately 18 percent of the city's population are of Maroon descent.

Principal festivities during the annual celebration of Maroon Day are held in Paramaribo where thousands of visitors also attend the events. Maroon Day begins with the customary Prodowaka Parade. This is a semi-formal procession where members of all Maroon nations demonstrate their historical and cultural heritage by playing the wutg drum, singing, and dancing while participants proceed through the city streets. The festivities also include other traditional Maroon music and dances along with speeches and tributes.

University of Suriname
Anton de Kom Universiteit van Suriname

The people of Suriname did not have access to post-secondary education until 1983 when the University of Suriname was established. The institution, located in Paramaribo, remains the only university of higher education in Suriname. University of Suriname includes faculties in the areas of medicine, social sciences, humanities, mathematical and physical sciences, along with technological sciences. A number of research centers are also located on the campus. While the university has continued to expand in Paramaribo, it has not centralized its academic offerings by introducing programs to extension sites in areas such as Maroon communities. Therefore, students living in other districts who qualify to attend the university must move to Paramaribo at their own expense.

The university, however, connects with the Maroon community so that students may better understand the cultural heritage of this indigenous group. For instance, with financial support, the university organized a study trip to Saramaccan villages with 21 students enrolled in the History of the Humanities class. The three-day study trip to the Upper Suriname area allowed students to become acquainted with the rich cultural heritage and the traditional authority of the Saramaccans. Students and professors made a courtesy visit to the chief captain who is also the chairman of the Association of Saramaccan Authorities. The students gave him a gift with the inscription "ADEK University". Visits were also made to the Saramaccan museum and to Totomboti, the workshop of the Rastafarian Artistic Collective. In addition, the visit included a viewing of the traditional construction style of the Saramaccans in Pikin Slee. The study trip was concluded with a visit to the Saamaccan village of Botopasi. The university has also taken an interest in providing information on African culture by holding conferences that include the history of slavery. Furthermore, a professor is assigned to dedicate time to conducting research on the Maroon culture and sharing knowledge through teachings and writings.

South American Journey

South America
and Education

Approximately 10 million enslaved Africans were transported to the New World between 1518 and 1873. From reports, the Portuguese brought 3.5 million Africans to Brazil to work on sugar and coffee plantations as well as in the mines. This is considered the largest number of slaves transported from African nations to any one colonial territory. The number represented 40 percent of the Atlantic slave trade, six to seven times more than the number of slaves transported to the United States. Another 200,000 slaves were imported to Colombia, and they also labored on sugar plantations and in gold mines. Ecuador received an estimate of 200,000 slaves too. Peru, Venezuela, Argentina, Uruguay, and Paraguay each received a total of 100,000 Africans who worked not only on sugar plantations but also as dock hands, miners, household workers, and field hands in various agricultural ventures. Around 30,000 slaves were transported to Bolivia to perform excessive, dangerous work in mines. Not all slaves brought to South America came from Africa since a number of them arrived from British colonies during the later years of slavery. Nevertheless, during the slavery era and thereafter, South America maintained an intricate system of racial classification of the Africans and their descendants

Some enslaved people could write, and others could read but not write. Those who could not read or write found someone who would write on their behalf. They frequently turned to friends or asked members of groups such as the confraternities, the free Black Militias, or the African Nations. In the case of the Black Militias, most captains were literate. They could read or they had some capacity to write. On the record, a member of the militia, Molina, reported that as a militiaman during the 1790s, he was asked by the white inspector general of the militias to teach some of his fellow Black militiamen how to read. This was surprising to Molina because such a request was not acceptable to the colonial regime.

In South America, the education gap is a duplicate of the income gap between rich and poor. According to Worldfund, 74 million South Americans, an estimate of 12.4 percent of the region's population, live on less than $2 per day, and over half of them are children. Ranked on the bottom income quintile, children complete an average of 8 years of school versus over 10 years completed by children in the top income quintile. For those children living below the poverty line, access to quality education in South America is uncommon and challenging to attain. Worldfund notes that investment in education is generally directed to high-income students.

Brazil
Education During and After Slavery

Education was reserved for the privileged, but no law was enacted in Brazil to prohibit slaves from learning to read and write. In fact, many of the Muslim Minas from Africa came to Brazil as highly educated slaves even more so than many of their Portuguese owners who were illiterate (Akande, 2016). Some municipalities enacted laws that obligated slave-owners to teach slaves how to read and write so they could "feed their souls of the revealed Word of Our Lord and save their lifes". So, some slaves and freed Brazilians became proficient in reading and writing Portuguese. However, establishing a public-school system to provide formal education to freed slaves after emancipation was not forthcoming.

According to McLucas (2005), Afro-Brazilians make up approximately 50 percent of the country's entire population and 70 percent of these Brazilians live below the poverty line. In this type of environment, many children do not receive adequate education to progress to post-secondary institutions or enter Brazil's white-collar workforce. McLucas (2005) quotes from Walker's NACLA Report on the Americas that education has a much lower rate of completion amongst Afro-Brazilians across all levels. Many do not finish past the grade 4 for reasons such as the need to begin working to support the family. According to the 2002 Brazilian National Census, Afro-Brazilians, 15 years or older experience more than twice the illiteracy rate than white Brazilians and are twice as likely to drop out of school than their white counterparts not only because they have to work, but also they do not believe that going to school will do much for them (Cottrol, 2013). Afro-Brazilian students receive, on average, five hours of education per day at public schools. On the other hand, their white counterparts, the majority of whom attend private schools, receive eight hours of education per day. Furthermore, in spite of education quotas, many Afro-Brazilians attending inner-city secondary schools are still not able to attend universities because the standard of public education they receive does not sufficiently prepare them to successfully complete the university entrance exams.

After completing elementary school, Afro-Brazilian students may choose to attend a secondary school where curriculum includes at least one foreign language, philosophy, sociology, geography, history, physics, chemistry, biology, mathematics, art and physical education. Those who complete their studies will receive a graduation certificate that will allow them to take the university entrance exam. After completing elementary school, students also have the option of attending a vocational secondary school. The curriculum at the vocational school may include general as well as specialized vocational subjects. Students graduate with a technical certificate or diploma. In addition to secondary and vocational secondary education, Afro-Brazilians may choose to take adult education secondary school diploma classes for non-traditional students. After graduating, these students may sit the university entrance exams. Students may also attend secondary schools that include elementary level II which allows enrollment from grade 7 until graduation.

In 2001, Brazil's federal government passed laws to address racial and socioeconomic inequalities that prevented Afro-Brazilian students from entering state and federal universities throughout the years. At that time, the president responded to pressure, especially from Afro-Brazilian feminist and social movements. He established an affirmative action policy that set quotas to increase access to public services and universities for Afro-Brazilians and other groups who had been disenfranchised by unfair limitations (Aubel, 2011). Rio de Janeiro became the first Brazilian state to adopt quotas for Afro-Brazilian students at institutions of higher education in 2002. By 2010, roughly 150 of the country's 2,000 higher education institutions had adopted some form of affirmative action. Despite a few instances when some whites claimed to be of Afro-Brazilian descent or connected to another minority race, the quotas had worked at these universities because it enabled equal access to education. But, in opposition to the quotas, two separate court challenges were made by critics of affirmative action. However, on April 16, 2012, The Law of Status Quota was passed unanimously by the Brazilian Supreme Court that ruled affirmative action policies can take a person's race into consideration for university admittance. The court found the use of racial quotas constitutional, allowing both the 59 public universities to reserve a certain percentage of slots for Afro-Brazilians, biracial citizens, and Amerindian undergraduate students coming from public secondary schools. The law states that by 2016, 50 percent of spaces at the public universities must go to students from families with incomes below $503 per month and that half of those slots must be allocated to students of Afro-Brazilian, biracial, or Amerindian race. The Law of Status Quota has served its purpose in guaranteeing equal access to education and a better future for so many disenfranchised students.

The initial affirmative action recipients expressed that they encountered problems at universities since the quotas failed to take their financial needs into consideration. These recipients did not believe they were prepared socially to enter university, and the institutions were not conscious of the social realities of affirmative action. Many of these recipients came from poor backgrounds, so the cost of living for them was extremely high without scholarships. As a result, some struggled to stay at universities and eventually dropped out. They believed that more attention should have been paid to orienting recipients and the university community about the social realities of attending as a full-time student.

The Federal University of Bahia is located in Salvador, the capital city of the state of Bahia. It has the largest concentration of Afro-Brazilians and others of African descent. As the major university in the state, it serves approximately 18,000 students. However, according to Aldridge & Yates (2000), there were no Afro-Brazilian professors or Africana classes as late as 2000. During the same year, the University of Sao Paulo had a few Afro-Brazilian professors and students, but no Afro-Brazilian or Africana classes at the prestigious university. Both universities are examples that even when located in areas with a high Afro-Brazilian population, leaders at these institutions had made no effort to diversify the student and faculty population. Such practices indicate why there was a great need for racial quotas. But, even with racial quotas, white students, including those from affluent families, continue to represent the majority student population at the public universities. Many of their parents can afford to pay for them to attend private secondary school and take extra classes to receive rigorous preparations to pass the university entrance test. This is contrary to Afro-Brazilians who have to contend with sub-standard secondary education.

Bahia

Portuguese colonists bought a vast number of slaves to work on their sugar plantations in the state of Bahia in northeastern Brazil. Many of the slaves' descendants still call the state their home. In fact, Salvador, the capital of Bahia, is regarded as the city in Brazil that is most representative of the African continent's population (Instituto Brasil África, 2017). The city has a population of approximately 3 million residents with over 80 percent of African heritage. In the city, the largest number of Afro-Brazilians reside in the Liberdade neighborhood. This neighborhood of 600,000 residents is regarded as having the highest number Afro-Brazilians living in one location in the country. Liberdade became known during the late 19th century when the area was assigned specifically for the execution of slaves and convicts. The name came about because many slaves resigned themselves to the hopeless thought that death was the only way of escape to achieve their liberty (liberdade).

Since Salvador has a large Afro-Brazilian population, residents have maintained practices of their slave ancestors which is noticeable in their food, religion, music, dance, art and other cultural habits. The vibrant culture is also seen in the popular festivals that are held each year in Salvador.

In spite of the well-known status of Salvador, it is one of the cities where there are drastic socio-economic disparities between Brazilians of European descent and those of African ancestry including biracial residents. In fact, Bahia is one of the poorer and less developed states as compared to the southern states (Cottrol, 2013).

Colegio Estadual Manoel Devoto

Colegio Estadual Manoel Devoto's opening in 1957 was long-awaited by residents in Salvador who did not previously have access to secondary education. From its opening, the school has served not only children living in Rio Vermelho and its surrounding areas, but also those living in distant neighborhoods such as Barra, Vitória, Chame-chame, and Rio Mouth. Approximately 1,800 Afro-Brazilian and biracial students between the ages of 15 and 20 years, from various socioeconomic backgrounds, make up the majority of students enrolled at the school named after a great Bahian educator. To accommodate so many students, they are assigned to one of three shifts where they interact with a staff of about 106 teachers and administrators. In addition to 25 classrooms, there are sports courts, a science lab, a computer room, a library, a video room and an auditorium that can accommodate a capacity of 200 persons. Students participate in games and gymnastics. The school also hosts outside events such as dances, music concerts, and futsal ball team competitions.

The school's Student Guild has united various student social groups. The guild establishes rules and rights of: students, projects and agendas, plus school activities. Through the Student Guild, students are encouraged to form student movements to engage in activism in support of Afro-Brazilian culture along with women and LGBT rights. The guild also urges students to fight against racism.

On a number of occasions, students have been active in shutting down the school's operations so as to advocate for the poor working conditions of teachers and support staff. In addition, they demonstrated against the deteriorating buildings at the school. Furthermore, students staged a walk out of classes against overcrowding that left insufficient classroom space for the large student population. Their grievances also included undrinkable water, dirty bathrooms, the non-payment and dismissal of support staff, among other concerns. Student activism not only disrupted class attendance, but it ultimately brought public attention to the government's neglect of the school for so many years.

Feira de Santana State College

The Feira de Santana State College was opened as the Normal School and State Gymnasium of Feira de Santana on March 5, 1949 to those living in the predominantly Afro-Brazilian and biracial community of Feira de Santana, Bahia. On November 11, 1957, the then governor of Bahia made a decree for all gymnasiums to be transformed into colleges. The steady increase of enrollment at the Feira de Santana State College resulted in a need to construct a larger building. Junior courses were taught in the new Feira de Santana State College building while gymnasium/collegiate courses continued to be taught at the original normal school building until classes were discontinued. The Feira de Santana State College became a community school where elementary, middle, and vocational classes were taught until the mid-1990s when the elementary and vocational courses were discontinued, and the school was converted into a secondary school. This change from catering to a wide student population caused a decline in enrollment. However, today, the school has reclaimed its community school status since it caters not only to secondary school levels, but it accepts both grade 5 elementary students and adult education learners. The re-introduction of elementary and adult education has caused an increase once again in the total student enrollment.

The level of student learning has remained very low throughout the years as a result of the educational disadvantages that have plagued Afro-Brazilians and biracial learners since slavery. Students continue to experience difficulties with reading, interpreting, logical reasoning, and concentration. In addition, the behavior of some students has been influenced by community issues such as drugs, harassment, and family problems. But the school has continued to overcome challenges with the help of community assisted projects. Moreover, some students do not allow their negative surroundings to affect their learning since many have successfully completed both the university entrance exams and the selective processes to enter the job market. In addition, more students have been participating in socio-educational and extra-class activities in spite of their school shifts and transportation issues. Teachers are also a motivating influence because they encourage students to participate in leadership and other positive student extra-curriculum activities that help to build their character which ultimately influences their perceptions of learning.

The University of International Integration of Afro-Brazilian Lusophony, Bahia

The University of International Integration of Afro-Brazilian Lusophony (Unilab) was established as a federal, public university in São Francisco do Conde, Bahia in July 2010. São Francisco do Conde is formerly a part of Salvador, but it is now an independent municipality with a census count of over 90 percent Afro-Brazilian residents. Unilab's Bahia campus was opened in February 2013. The inaugural class of 3,000 students enrolled in various undergraduate courses. Postgraduate face-to-face classes on campus started in May 2014 in the areas of teaching, research, and continuing education.

The common theme of the university is to collaborate with other Portuguese-speaking countries, specifically from the continent of Africa. Academic programs are introduced at the university to stimulate economic, political, and social growth among students and thereby provide them with an ability to impart their knowledge on others. One expectation is also to introduce advanced education to Afro-Brazilians in the interior parts of the northeastern region. Along with the main campus, other campuses include Auroras, Palmares and Redenção /CE, the birthplace of the abolition of slavery.

Rio de Janeiro

Approximately one million slaves were transported to Rio de Janeiro. In this 21st century, it is common to see a large population of Afro-Brazilians living in poverty-stricken areas known as favelas or slums throughout Rio de Janeiro. The favelas were established since the final years of the 19th century when squatter settlements began to develop. From that period, many living in countryside towns relocated to the city in search of work. Due to the lack of affordable housing, they settled in unlivable conditions that eventually developed into the favelas of today. The first Afro-Brazilians settled in these areas in homes at the base of the hillside because at this location they were more likely to have electricity and running water. So, further up the hillside the newer shanty dwellings have less access to necessities.

Large families often reside in a one-room houses with narrow, cramped spaces in between each unit. The overcrowding, lack of running water, and accumulation of sewage create health problems for residents. Clinics and other health care facilities, when they exist, are also overcrowded and poorly equipped. Some favela residents must also contend with heavy rains that carry garbage down the hillsides and create landslides that wash away flimsy housing.

As migration steadily increased to the favelas, a growing urban underclass began to organize internally by forming their own favela associations since city and state governments failed to provide many public services. While residents worked together to provide sanitation, medical care, and transportation in their communities, they have had to rely on the government to construct public schools. Elementary schools are located throughout favelas, but many of these densely populated communities still do not have secondary schools. Therefore, many students still must travel elsewhere, even long journeys, to complete their secondary school education. The Rio das Pedras favela has one public high school; Maré in the North Zone has none as of this writing. City of God did not have any high schools until recent years when construction began, but the work was stopped temporarily due to political conflicts.

Early migrants to Rio de Janeiro and their descendants have become trapped by not only poverty and crime but also the cycle of low standard education and limited resources to support their learning. Students at many favela schools have to contend with outdated, unengaging curriculum, and some teaching methods have not evolved from its traditional format. Teacher qualifications are another concern because many new teachers are not prepared when they are assigned to favela schools. The high illiteracy rate that exists from such low level for education for most Afro-Brazilian children has resulted in difficulties of some students in passing the rigorous tests to enter public universities or finding employment.

Colegio Estadual Journalist Tim Lopes

Colegio Estadual Journalist Tim Lopes was a well needed welcome for a community with a large secondary student population. The school was opened in 2011 in the slums of Alemão complex in the suburb of Rio de Janeiro. It has an enrollment of approximately 1,800 students who are assigned to three shifts. After neglecting to provide adequate funding for secondary education for centuries, students in the Alemão complex now have an opportunity to attend a state-of-the-art high school in their own community that encompasses a positive learning environment. The school has 15 classrooms, air-conditioned spaces, a swimming pool, a sports court, game rooms, laboratories, a library, and auditoriums. The institution also provides accessibility to Wi-Fi network with connections to the education system. State-of-the-art video equipment is available in the cafeteria, multimedia room, multi-functional and meeting rooms. In addition to serving the learning needs of children, the campus is also used for teacher training workshops. The facilities also provide a location for community workshops. Furthermore, other community events are held at the school from time to time.

The school was named after Tim Lopes, an investigative journalist and producer for the Brazilian television network. He was murdered in 2002 by traffickers from the Vila Cruzeiro favela, in the Alemão complex of Rio de Janeiro. He was working undercover to do a report on child sexual abuse and drug trafficking when he was abducted and tortured. So, located in the heart of the shanty town where Tim Lopes was murdered, the secondary school has its challenges. It is affected by a high crime rate and other disruptive occurrences within the community. Moreover, there have been break-ins leading to theft of valuable school property. Also, unauthorized use of the school's facilities is common, and this problem has even resulted in the death of a child. Nevertheless, students are aware of the importance the school plays in the community. They have gotten involved in activism such as marching in the streets in support of a teachers' strike and also voicing their need for the government to provide them with better education.

Colegio Estadual Jornalista Mauício Azêdo

The Maurício Azêdo Journalist College is located in the favela of Caju, Rio de Janeiro. The area was deprived of a government secondary school until consideration was given to renovate a structure in the Caju Olympic Village. The school was opened in 2016. It serves all residents of Boa Esperança Park and 12 other surrounding communities. The high school stands out as a model institution because it provides students with dual enrollment courses that allow them to complete academic requirements and, at the same time, be trained as logistics technicians. The training has provided students with skills for gainful employment once they graduate. The logistics program is conducted in partnership with various corporate entities and government agencies involved in logistics. Students are trained by the National Industrial Apprenticeship Service (SENAI). The classes are full time with approximately 250 students. This is a low enrollment number in contrast to the commonly overcrowded student population at many favela schools where a shift system is required.

The school previously achieved academic excellence with the exceptional performance of two students who were awarded honorable mention for level 3 at the 12th Brazilian Mathematics Olympiad of Public Schools (OBMEP). Another accomplishment is that the school was chosen by The State Department of Education to launch a meditation pilot project. Moreover, it was the first school in Rio de Janeiro to include meditation classes in the curriculum. The project was intended to improve student performance and ease stress, anxiety, and difficulty concentrating. The pilot initiative became so popular that it attracted interest and enrollment of many students throughout the school.

The downside of Maurício Azêdo Journalist College is that it is located in a high crime area and is impacted despite the presence of the Pacifying Police Unit (UPP). Most of the students have a story to tell of the violence they have experienced at home or at school. The community's 20,000 residents live in a dangerous environment with armed traffickers. Unfortunately, the school's location is right in the line of gun fire when there are clashes between police and criminals. The bullet holed walls in nine classrooms was a constant psychological reminder and created a sense of fear in both students and teachers who are constantly aware that the school is not a safe place. In fact, there are days when students, teachers, and other staff members have had to lie face-down on the floor while shootings are occurring. Furthermore, the gun battles have caused the school to close from time-to-time which hinders the students' learning progress.

Maranhão

Maranhão, located in the dense rainforest, is the third Brazilian state with the largest percentage of Afro-Brazilian population. According to the Instituto Brasileiro de Geografia e Estatística or Brazilian Institute of Geography and Statistics, Maranhão has approximately 4.5 million Afro-Brazilians. They represent more than 74 percent of the state's population. The state is known for its vibrant culture in religion, music, and other culture that have been passed down from slaves who were captured from different parts of the African continent to work on plantations in Maranhão. One of the popular celebrations in Maranhão is the fiesta, which includes the sounds from vigorous drumming to creole music. The laid-back, conscious rhythm of reggae music is also prominent during that festivity.

The African traditions are evident in São Luís, the state's largest city and capital. It is recognized for its cultural resources from a legacy of slavery. The medium-sized city has a population of approximately 500,000 - 1,000,000 residents. Traditional celebrations have transformed São Luís into one of the Brazilian cities where African religion, culture, music, and cuisine have a strong influence on residents and visitors.

Universidade Federal do Maranhão

Universidade Federal do Maranhão (UFMA) was founded in São Luis, Maranhão in 1966. It is a non-profit, public higher education institution. Programs are accredited by Brazil's Ministry of Education. UFMA has a selective admission's policy based on entrance examinations. The institution offers courses and programs leading to bachelors and master's degrees in various areas of study. It also provides several academic and non-academic courses off-campus, online, and through distance learning.

Maranhão is recognized as the first Brazilian state to offer an undergraduate degree in African and Afro-Brazilian studies. The program is located on the UFMA campus and was approved by the Ministry of Education. The course prepares public school teachers to teach African history and culture in elementary and secondary schools. The African and Afro-Brazilian program at UFMA is a four-year course and has a target of recruiting a maximum of 40 students.

The government-funded program includes topics that cover social and race-based inequalities throughout Brazil.

The initiative for starting the program at UFMA developed from a need to enforce the 2013 federal law for the compulsory teaching of African history and culture in schools. However, the process of starting African and Afro-Brazilian programs has not been readily embraced at other public universities. Implementing the curriculum elsewhere has been slow so has resulted in insufficient teachers for that subject area. Opponents of the program argue that the subject is already covered in either one or other disciplines such as history of Africa and/or diversity education. It is speculated that the opposition sabotaged any consideration, development, and recruitment efforts for the program to be implemented at other public universities. Supporters are concerned that brief inclusion of topics on African and Afro-Brazilian history and culture in other curriculum is not enough to change stereotypical, isolated views on Africans and the Afro-Brazilian population for years to come. Furthermore, supporters are troubled that such vague coverage of the topic in schools will not address the prejudice and racist attitudes that continue to exist at universities. Nevertheless, educators teaching the program at UFMA continue be optimistic that other public higher education institutions will take their lead and start African and Afro-Brazilian programs to provide teachers with knowledge to educate students on this topic inside the classrooms.

São Paulo

Slaves transported to São Paulo were initially the sole labor force working on sugar plantations. A larger labor force of both slaves and freed Afro-Brazilian was necessary when the sugar industry declined and was replaced by a booming coffee industry. Its additional workforce came from outside of Brazil with an influx of overseas laborers. As a result, the population surged in São Paulo, and the increase transformed the town into a major city.

São Paulo became known not only as the major producer of Brazilian coffee but also for its Afro-Brazilian activism. As early as the 1930s, the Black Brazilian Front (Frente Negra Brasileira) was established in the city. Although this group was started in São Paulo, it had affiliates in several states in Brazil, including Bahia and Rio Grande Sul. The group was one of the first civil rights organizations to fight for and defend the Afro-Brazilian population. It was also the first organization to enter Afro-Brazilians as candidates to run for political office. None of the organization's candidates was elected for political office. However, other important projects of the organization were starting a school and advocating on behalf of many Afro-Brazilians for their civil rights. One instance of the organization's tireless fight for racial equality was their efforts in integrating a skating rink in São Paulo. Also, the group worked with Afro-Brazilians to obtain jobs in the public sector of São Paulo. Today, a combined population of Afro-Brazilians and bi-racial residents represent the second largest group of the 20 million residents in São Paulo, the largest city in Brazil and Latin America. Yet, consistent, blatant racism continues to be evident in employment, education, housing, and other instances throughout the city.

São Paulo is the richest state in Brazil Yet, it has the largest number of favelas and the highest number of people living in them which accounts for 3 million residents. Afro-Brazilians and the biracial population form the majority of residents in the favelas of São Paulo, which depicts a symbol of poverty and inequality in that city. According to Chiodelli (n.d.) during the 1980s, informal housing started to increase in São Paulo due to the economic crisis which struck the city and caused a rapid growth of unemployment and poverty. Consequently, many were forced to occupy dilapidated, informal settlements in not only favelas but also cortices - single room rentals in sub-divided houses with one bathroom. São Paulo's slums are usually characterized as: overcrowded in unhealthy environment with inadequate public spaces and facilities; constructed inappropriately in environmental risky and illegal locations; located a distance from central areas; and plagued by high levels of violence. Seventy percent of the favelas and the corticos are legally connected to the city's electricity, gas, and garbage collection network (Chiodelli n.d.). Approximately 56 percent of these dilapidated structures are connected to the sewerage system.

Universidade da Cidadania Zumbi dos Palmares (Unipalmares)

Universidade da Cidadania Zumbi dos Palmares, also known as Unipalmares or FAZP, was founded in the state of São Paulo in 2004. It has provided an affordable ray of hope for so many disenfranchised Afro-Brazilians and biracial people residing in and around São Paulo who could not enroll in the state's university. Named after a 17th century resistance leader, Unipalmares is privately owned by the Afro-Brazilian Institute of Higher Education. One of the main objectives of the institution is to reduce the higher education inequalities between Afro-Brazilians and whites since data from the 2012 Census of Higher Education indicates that only 13 percent of students attending higher education are Afro-Brazilians. Approximately 87 percent of Unipalmares's student population are descendants of African slaves. Most of the students work during the day time and attend classes on the busy campus during the evenings where they feel at home in a respectful learning environment. By 2012, with 1,400 graduates, the population of the only Afro-Brazilian university in the southern most region increased to approximately 1,600 students. The population increase triggered the move to facilities with larger and better learning accommodations.

In the beginning, 200 students enrolled in the business administration program. Offerings were subsequently expanded to five programs that included law and education. Another later program option was engineering with a specialty in transportation or oil and gas. Unipalmares has increased its academic offerings to ten programs. Students may also enroll in post-graduate courses. Attention is not only given to teaching the standard academic subjects, but students may also engage in a curriculum that includes classes associated with the institution's mission of defending minorities and the history of Africa.

All the classrooms at Unipalmares are named after famous people of African descent such as their own countryman, comedian Mussum. Classrooms are also named after famous people from the United States such as presenter Oprah Winfrey, activist Malcolm X, and President Barack Obama whose portrait hangs on a wall of the college. In addition to the portrait, a photo exhibition was held in honor of the first U.S. Afro-American president. Its wall was covered with a prominent print of President Obama's well-known slogan, "Yes, we can!"
Afro-Brazilian professors make up the majority of faculty on campus. Some of them and students participated in an exchange program with Xavier University, one of the historically Black universities in the United States. This was a short-term exchange program that targeted racism and human rights educational issues in Brazil and the United States.

Colombia
Education During and After Slavery

African slaves were legally banned from receiving an education. However, those who attended church in their communities learned about morality and received limited catechism from the clergy. The law was passed in 1821 to make primary education compulsory. But, the stalled construction of primary schools resulted in many freed slaves and their immediate descendants not learning to read or write. After the construction of limited schools, the compulsory education law remained irrelevant to the majority of Afro-Colombians who were unable to attend because of the lack of teachers, poverty, and other issues. The educational injustices to Afro-Colombians condemned them throughout generations to settle for the lowest paying jobs without any possibility of economic advancement from the bottom of the social ladder. On the other hand, children of some wealthy bi-racial proprietors, merchants, or administrators were taught reading, writing, and arithmetic. A few of those children, too, had more opportunities to continue their studies at colleges so that they could prepare themselves for careers that required a higher-education degree. Educational opportunities fulfilled the aspirations of those graduates to work in professions such as the clergy and law.

Buenaventura is an example of a palenque or town with an 80 percent Afro-Colombian population. The significant school drop-out rate in this town is attributed to various reasons. However, the primary reasons relate not only to poverty and crime but also to the lack of easy access to schools, especially in Buenaventura's deep rural areas. The highest level of education for many in Buenaventura is elementary school with 86 percent of the population completing this level (Herrera, 2012). In addition, 49 percent of the population received a secondary school diploma, 23 percent completed some other form of education, and 11 percent had access to higher education (CONPES 2006; DANE 2005 as noted in Herrera, 2012). The quality of education in this and similar cities are regarded as below standard so, as a result, the majority of these schools are considered low performing.

Data from the 2005 census confirms that the illiteracy rate of Afro-Colombian was 4.5 percent which was double that of the national percentage of 2.4 percent. That report indicates that 10 percent of children between 6 and 10 years old do not attend any school and 27 percent were not enrolled in secondary education at the time data was collected. (Rodríguez, Alfonso Rodríguez, Alfonso and Cavelier, 2009).

Palenque de San Basilio, Bolivar Province

Palenque de San Basilio is an isolated town in the foothills of Montes de Maria, Bolivar Province. Since the 15th century, palenques, or walled towns, served as hideouts for Maroons who escaped slavery and took refuge remote locations by building fortresses to barricade themselves against Spanish troops. Palenque San Basilio was founded by fugitive slaves who regrouped after escaping from the destruction of other palenques. Benkos Bioho was one of these fugitive slaves who made his way to Palenque San Basilio. As one of the palenque's leaders, Bioho formed an alliance with other run-away slaves and organized the escape of other slaves who all joined together as an army to fight against Spanish troops. Bioho later signed a peace treaty with the Spaniards but that decree was rescinded two years prior to Bioho's execution in 1621. In 1713, the Spanish Crown issued a Royal Decree officially pardoning those slaves who settled in Palenque de San Basilio to prevent the leaders from continuing to free and harbor runaway slaves. This made them the first free Africans in the Americas, and it lacks modern infrastructures.

While Palenque de San Basilio has stood the test of time as the last surviving palenque, it lacks modern infrastructures. For instance, the roads in Palenque de San Basilio have remained unpaved, and these dirt roads with pot holes are impassable. The houses do not have any better appearance as approximately half of the dwellings are made with rough brick and old paint. Electricity was not introduced into the town until the 1970s, and at an average temperature of 30° C or 86° F, there is usually no air conditioning for many. Palenque de San Basilio gives the impression of an abandoned village if it were not for the vibrant movements of its residents. According to the United Nations, 76 percent of these residents live today as slaves to poverty. Nevertheless, an aqueduct was constructed during the 1970s to direct water to the town. This construction eventually resulted in a funded project to build outside bathrooms onto housing premises.

Palenque de San Basilo appears to be the only town whose residents were not displaced by armed rebels during the initial years of the civil war. However, during the 2000s the remote town was not exempt from violence and displacement from not only rebels but the Colombian government. Despite this setback, residents continue to fight permanent battles to preserve the town's long-standing identity and culture. As a result, the village is regarded as the foundation and proof of the richness of African culture that is dominant in the mountainous Colombian territory. The town's isolation has allowed it to maintain its ethnic practices that include recognition as the only residents in the African diaspora of the Americas who have maintained their Creole language combined with

Spanish vocabulary. The town has been declared by UNESCO as a rare cultural heritage of humanity. Women vendors have continued to maintain the culture and sustain the local economy by making crafts and also by selling the traditional cocadas or sweets which are a type of pastry made from sugar and sesame seeds.

In the 1991 Colombian Constitution, a long-awaited formal recognition was made of Afro-Colombian ethnicity and the right of Afro-Colombian communities to claim title to the land they have traditionally worked on from generation to generation. But this recognition was paper based only since residents in Palenque de San Basilio and other towns do not have titles to the land they and their ancestors have resided on for centuries.

Institucion Educativa Técnica Agropecuaria Benkos Bioho de San Basilio De Palenque

Institucion Educativa Técnica Agropecuaria Benkos Bioho de San Basilio De Palenque (INSETABP) was initially known as the Mixed Departmental School of San Basilio de Palenque. INSETABP includes a combined population of approximately 800 students who attend either the town's only primary school or the technical secondary school situated at different locations in the community. At the technical secondary school, students specialize in agricultural courses. The learning they have acquired has positively impacted the agricultural needs in their farming community. Athletics is another important part of the school's curriculum.

The palenquera community leaders recognized during the mid-1980s that stigmatized residents began to abandon their culture due to shame and fear. This meant for leaders that they had to rescue and revive the town's culture to avoid any possibilities of it becoming extinct. The effort was made possible with the collaboration of the community and INSETABP to educate students on their palenquera culture. The first step to address the cultural concerns for community leaders was to conduct research in conjunction with the Ministry of National Education to learn about their own background of palenquera traditions from their own perspective without having the vision of people who were not part of their community. The research process provided information for the development of a new culturally based curriculum to replace the former that was implemented throughout the country. The outcome from research and discussions was that Afro-Colombian history would be taught at INSETABP rather than Colombian history; the palenquera language would be introduced into the curriculum rather than Spanish; and classes in the use of traditional medicinal options would be incorporated in natural science classes. The community, education ministry, and other stakeholders have continued to work towards common resolutions through forum to ensure that students at INSETABP receive cultural education.

In the age of technology, teachers from INSETABP were trained to use computers so they, in turn, could teach students to use electronic tablets that were donated in a partnership between the Colombian and Bolivian governments. After both schools were wired for internet signal, each student was given a tablet loaded with educational programs. Another high note for INSETABP occurred in 2016 when it was awarded first place in the annual school agricultural competition for its student project on the use of traditional medicine. The school has also continued to do well in athletic competitions.

The education of students at INSETABP was interrupted when it was closed for six months in 2000. At that time, the school premises served as a displacement site for neighboring residents of Mampujan who sought refuge during the civil war between government soldiers and armed rebels. The school facilities were overcrowded with approximately 57 families who came along with their livestock. They were forced to survive on the school compounds with the crops they brought from their farms. The students' learning was disrupted once again years later due to various issues such as unmaintained sanitary facilities that were in deplorable condition; poor drinkable water service; and abandoned classrooms due to flooding. The government in association with the Mixed Fund for the Promotion of Culture and Arts of Bolívar joined forces on a project to repair infrastructure at the school. Four classrooms plus the computer room were demolished in December 2011, with the intention of quickly rebuilding to return to normalcy at INSETABP. Since the construction was abruptly suspended, some classes were taught indefinitely outside, causing students to endure high temperatures and no sanitary services. Work later resumed to provide students, teachers, and administrators with new facilities.

Quibdó, Choco Province

Quibdó is the capital city of the province of Choco, which is considered the poorest province in Colombia. The climate of the city is extremely humid due to its location in the isolated, dense rainforest, also known as one of the rainiest areas of the world. The city is located near to the Atrato River where fishing has become one of the livelihoods of the residents who are overwhelming 95 percent Afro-Colombian descendants of slaves transported to the region to work in the gold mines.

Every year in Quibdó the popular San Pacho Festival is celebrated. During that time, residents and tourists come together for two weeks of fun and raucous revelries. Residents in each neighborhood design and make their own grand costumes which they wear while dancing in the street parade.

Residents in Quibdó and the surrounding villages suffered mentally and physically for many years from the violent clashes between the national troops and the FARC guerillas who used the western jungle locations, occupied by Afro-Colombians and indigenous Indian groups, for their hideouts and to house their kidnapped victims. This lengthy five-decade old war led to abuses that included killings, disappearances, kidnappings, tortures, forced displacements, attempted forced recruitments, planting landmines, extortions, and death threats against community leaders without protection from the Colombian government.

The central downtown area of the city is developed with well-maintained paved roads, buildings, businesses, a park, and pedestrian walk-paths. But, despite these developments, the residents of Quibdó and other Choco communities are grappling with long-standing issues including blatant government corruption that causes the delay in building and repairing infrastructure. Also, residents must contend with a poor garbage disposal system and the inferior health services with a nearly bankrupt hospital. Dirt roads and wooden shacks are still common throughout the city's outskirts where many reside and continue to live in poverty. Some families still do not have electricity or running water. Furthermore, Quibdó does not have roads that connect the capital to other major towns in the Colombian interior. Up until the writing of this book, people of Quibdó and the neighboring villages have been going to the streets to demonstrate against the deplorable conditions they face daily due to the Colombian government's neglect.

Institucion Educativa Femenina de Ensenaza Media y Professional

Institucion Educativa Femenina de Ensenaza Media y Professional (IEFEMP) was founded in Quibdó, Choco in 1934. Prior to the school's opening, the stereotypical perception of Afro-Colombian girls was that instead of going to school, they should do domestic housework or care for children or do manual labor. On the other hand, some progressive minded people believed that these girls needed to be trained not only to do domestic work, but they should also be engaged in academic studies.

IEFEMP began under the name Intendencial de Señoritas with two students. The institution later became known as Pedagogical Female Institute in 1948 when it was transformed into both a secondary and a normal teaching institution. Up until 1952 the school was controlled by the Choco Department of Education. Later, the administrative duties were transferred to the Ministry of National Education. In 1953, the first set of teachers graduated. After that year, the institution merged with the Women's Baccalaureate and Commerce High School, the Pedagogical Women's Institute, and the Polytechnic Institute. Under the leadership of Catholic nuns, the new name became Feminine Institute of Secondary and Professional Education. By 1957, the school was approved as a baccalaureate and commercial high school and underwent another name change to The Women's Institute of Secondary and Vocational Education. The school now provides a secondary school curriculum for approximately

300 girls. In addition, primary school classes are offered for younger girls, so the combined population is roughly 2,700 female students with 95 teachers. In addition to the general academic subjects, secondary school students may choose to specialize in areas of commerce or natural sciences or humanities or environment.

A school museum was opened on campus in 1997. The museum was opened in response to a need to maintain the cultural, historical, and social values of the Chocoano people. The historic site was intended to showcase ancestral knowledge, materials, culture, traditional practices and genetic heritage of the Chocoano people. Students, teachers, administrators, and all stakeholders in the community came together to contribute historical photos and artifacts to make it into a full-fledged museum. Exhibits from those efforts include invaluable artifacts from the African culture that transforms into historical testimony of the lives of slaves transported to the area. Documents contributed reveal the essence of African ancestors. Students and others visiting the museum can connect with their roots and be proud to identify as Chocoano people. The museum was recognized in 2002 as one of the national museums.

One of the main problems at the school is, at the time of writing, the student population has outgrown the auditorium seating limits so cultural, religious, or academic events with a capacity of 3,000 and over cannot be hosted there. These space limitations cause students to gather instead on the field in the heat or rainy conditions to see an event. In addition to this field, a larger outdoor recreational space is needs for students to participate in cultural, sports, or scientific activities.

Universidad Tecnologica Del Choco Diego Luis Cordoba (UTCH)

The Universidad Tecnologica Del Choco Diego Luis Cordoba (UTCH) is a public university located at the heart of the Afro-Colombian community in Quibdó, Choco. The school's namesake, Diego Luis Cordoba, was an advocate of Afro-Colombians, especially for their education at all levels. He believed they were entitled to every social advancement opportunity similar to their white counterparts. The planning of the university began in accordance with a decree in 1968. Diego Luis Cordoba Polytechnic Institute was opened in 1972 with an enrollment of 203 students and 24 professors. Residents of Quibdó welcomed the opening that addressed the long-standing advanced education needs of the majority Afro-Colombian population.

The inaugural class of students enrolled in one of the bachelors' degree programs that included studies in the languages, mathematics and physics, social sciences and economics, chemistry and biology, psychology, educational administration and business management technology. During the same year of the institution's inception, the name was changed to Universidad Tecnologica Del Choco Diego Luis Cordoba (UTCH) in agreement with a national law. The name change provided more opportunities on both the province and national levels that included the introduction of new programs. By 1984, student enrollment increased to 1,345 with the addition of agricultural technology, civil works, fishing, mining, and social work. In 1987, the introduction of distance education courses further increased the student population to 2000 with approximately 200 professors. The institution was officially recognized as a university in 1993. This higher education status increased the authority of the institution's leaders who were given the responsibility in 1994 of electing their president for the first time. UTCH began offering post graduate courses in 1997. Students had additional new course offerings to choose from in 1998.

In addition to course offerings on campus, students may also participate in educational exchange programs with universities in Colombia or universities in other countries. Also, workshops and diploma programs are conducted on and off campus. These workshops and diploma programs enable the university to provide educational opportunities to the community in collaboration with stakeholders such as: the city of Quibdó, Choco territories, the Pacific region, the coffee region, and designated municipalities in the Antioquia province. Moreover, the university offers a number of other community services including legal and business aid centers, career coaching, access to a library and archive services, a community radio station, the use of event venues, and access to scientific resources such as the herbarium.

As a research university with a current population of over 10,000 students and 900 faculty members, the campus is home to the Afro-Colombian and Indigenous Cultural Center, the Research Center for Flora, and the School of Arts of the Pacific. Apart from the construction of these centers and other academic buildings, the sports center is another structural accomplishment that is located on campus.

Venezuela
Education During and After Slavery

Information is limited on the schooling or non-schooling of slaves in Venezuela. However, after emancipation, children were involved in informal systems of education by watching and learning from parents and adults in the community. In 1935, less than 20 percent of the school aged 7-14 years old children were in school (Sanchez, 1963). Many Afro-Venezuelans were expected to be among the remaining 80 percent of the population who did not attend school because those highly populated districts with Afro-Venezuelan residents had limited or no schools. Those who attended the few schools in rural, mountainous areas would probably learn in one-room without furniture or a blackboard or instructional materials. These schools would often be assigned untrained teachers who were educated up to the fourth-grade. They attended the same school they were assigned to teach.

The privilege that a few received in obtaining an education was extended to all when education was later considered a human right. Sanchez, (1963) informs that during the late 1970s, Afro-Venezuelan children were transitioned into a more formal educational system that enabled them to attend up to grade 6. In addition, subsidized educational programs allowed more Afro-Venezuelans to enroll in elementary school, secondary school, and even college. These educational reforms permitted some Afro-Venezuelan students in rural communities to continue their formal education by moving to cities after graduating from grade 6. Education reforms were also geared towards those who dropped out of school. Massive literacy campaigns and adult education programs allowed more than 1.5 million adults to learn to read and write or to return to school. Further reforms were enacted in August 2009 that made a positive impact on the rights of Afro-Venezuelans. As such, five articles in the new Organic Law of Education were approved and one of the provisions opened the door to enacting new regulations that included teaching African history at educational institutions

As of 1999, former President Hugo Chavez introduced, in stages, a new school system called Bolivarian schools, named after Simón Bolivar. The educational aspect of Chavez's Bolivarian Revolution is associated with socialist reforms. Chavez's intentions were to provide equal education to all students by refurbishing buildings and constructing new schools for those disenfranchised Afro-Venezuelans and the indigenous population. Bolivarian schools countered years of neglect in educating those residing in impoverished ethnic communities. An aspect of the Bolivarian school curriculum has been for students to participate in a social impact community project where they not only learn about the history of their community but also participate in neighborhood activities such as agricultural projects or traditional crafts making.

The Bolivarian school system was also introduced in higher education with the opening of territorial universities as alternatives to public and private universities. These institutions have continued to cater to elites yet still receive major government funding. The new universities include the Experimental National University of Yaracuy; Maritime University of the Caribbean; National Experimental University of the Armed Forces (UNEFA); Experimental National University of South of the Lake and the Bolivarian University of Venezuela. Also, four new University Institutes of Technology were created which are: the IUT of Bolívar State, the IUT of Apure State, the IUT of Barinas State and the IUT in la Fría Táchira State. Local community colleges were converted to territorial universities with the intention that they would be an educational option to everyone.

The Bolivarian university system has an open-admissions process which allows all to enroll, regardless of prior educational experience, qualifications, or nationality. At the universities, students are able to select a variety of specialties such as science and technology, ergonomics, library research, public administration, applied computer sciences, food science, and other academic areas. In addition, students engage in projects that contribute to the local communities. Courses are not assigned to departments as is customary at traditional universities. Instead, a multidisciplinary approach to learning is implemented at the institutions. Classes may be taught by professors who do not hold traditional degrees but are employed for their wealth of knowledge and experiences. Therefore, those, especially from poor communities, who would never be considered for employment at traditional universities have opportunities to share their wisdom in academic settings.

Mission Sucre is an anti-poverty and social welfare program that is geared towards secondary school students who are classified within the poorest and most marginalized segments of society. The program provides them with free undergraduate and graduate level education. It was implemented by President Chávez in 2003 as one of the Bolivarian series of educational missions. The Mission Sucre policy has been expected to encourage its recipients to graduate within three years versus the usual five or more years at the traditional public and private universities. Certain courses, such as foreign languages, are eliminated from the curriculum. But the non-traditional curriculum is unique with accelerated programs such as physician studies where low-income students have opportunities to train to become licensed doctors.

The Bolivarian school system has been met with resistance from the elite class who regard the new structure as a threat to their academic freedom and institutional autonomy. These critics of the new institution have regarded the modern universities as an extension of the government's propaganda, Marxist doctrine. They were disturbed that Chavez's reforms caused severe underinvestment in the traditional public universities and their academic research funding. These resistances have been challenged by the government. Moreover, those in agreement with the government see the new system of education as a counter action to traditional values of university autonomy and exclusory practices.

La Sabana, Caruao, Vargas State

Caruao, popularly known as Parroquia Caruao, is made up of small Afro-Venezuelan populated towns that are scattered throughout the extreme east of the Vargas state. These rural, seaside towns include La Sabana, Chuspa, Osma, Oritapo, Todasana, and Caruao. La Sabana, is the capital of Caruao Parish and the largest populated town. Main businesses for the parish is located in La Sabana. This town was founded during the 17th century along with the community of Chuspa. In 1778, 56 out of 75 residents were freed slaves. By 1788, the population decreased, and only 24 former slaves remained. By 1802, the area became formally known as La Sabana, and its residents lived in eight to ten shacks. By 1990, the census indicated approximately 3,961 residents in La Sabana and throughout the remote Caruao region.

The community of La Sabana was initially one property divided by the landowner into four large estates or plantations for farming and cattle grazing. The land on the plantations was regarded as ideal for cultivating cocoa, so slaves were transported to the parish to work on properties where they grew cocoa under brutal conditions. In addition to cocoa, sugarcane became another economically important crop to grow in La Sabana during the 18th and 19th centuries. After emancipation, former slaves in the communities continued to farm these crops on a smaller scale despite the responsibilities and difficulties to maintain the crops. The parish is now known for producing cocoa of the highest quality.

An information center is located in La Sabana where residents may participate in workshops. Residents who participated in the National Technological Literacy workshop were provided with literacy manuals on technology and free software. This workshop included a practical course that reinforced the theory in the manuals they received. The newly acquired knowledge of using communications technology allowed those living in poverty-stricken towns to be better able to manage their communities' building projects. For instance, some used their knowledge to participate in the historical project of redesigning Caruao to make it appear similar to that of slavery and colonial era periods. For this project, residents collaborated with the Scientific and Humanistic Development Council and a research team of professors.

Caruao is influenced by its African culture. Musical instruments and food are examples of customs that have been passed down from one generation to the next. Other customs are the well-known commemorations that are celebrated annually in La Sabana. Festivities include Parrandas de San Juan, Velorio de Cruz, Velorio del Niño Jesús, and Parranda del Inocent.

Liceo Bolivariano Caruao

Liceo Bolivariano Caruao, situated in La Sabana, has an enrollment of approximately 565 students. Students reside throughout different rural areas of the Caruao Parish. The school serves as a community learning center where students not only engage in academic studies, but they also participate in external learning activities that relate to furthering their knowledge of the rich history of their community and its cultural impact in Venezuela. For example, under the coordination of the Pedagogical Ethics Movement, students celebrate Afro-Venezuelan Day. This day is recognized every May 10th and was initiated by President Chávez to eliminate racial discrimination in Venezuela. On that day, learning activities include bringing awareness to the bravery of Afro-Venezuelan heroes such as José Leonardo Chirinos. Students become familiar with other Afro-Venezuelan heroes who have impacted the Venezuelan society during slavery and the colonial era. Students also learn how contributions of the heroes continue to resonate throughout the country. Students expand their learning with activities where they can integrate knowledge and develop better understanding of their culture.

Students attending Liceo Bolivariano Caruao have benefitted from the school's partnership with private and government entities. For example, the Super @ Ulas Program was implemented at the school by CANtv, the government's telecommunications company. With the support of the Ministry of Education and Sports, the program provided students in this remote community with access to updated information technologies and communications which made it possible to use computers and the internet at school.

The school has its setbacks which includes instances when it is affected after heavy rains if the Caruao and La Sabana rivers overflow. At such times, La Sabana and the surrounding communities will be cut off if the temporary bridge collapses. The school has no recourse but to suspend classes until students are able to travel to school. Furthermore, throughout the years, the school has experienced ongoing problems with bus transportation for students to get to school. In one instance, boys from the school blocked the Caruao-La Sabana road in protest of the lack of transportation to get them to school because the only school bus broke down. The outraged students demanded a response from the government and continued with their protest that disrupted traffic from 7:00 AM to 3:00 PM until government authorities showed up. These students were instrumental in influencing a change when they reached an agreement for a temporary bus to be assignment to the school until the other bus was repaired.

La Escuela Técnica Industrial Prof. Carlos Fiol

Marapa Marina, in the Catia la Mar region of Vargas state, is another town with a high Afro-Venezuelan population. The town is recorded in the 2011 census as the fifth most densely populated region with Afro-Venezuelans. Students in Marapa Marina have an opportunity to learn technical skills at La Escuela Técnica Industrial Prof. Carlos Fiol. The school was opened on October 10, 1980 as the National Educational Unit, Las Tunitas Creation. It was founded in response to a need for a secondary school to educate children living in the adjacent town of Las Tunitas. The school was opened during the 1980 - 1981 school year with five classrooms, a laboratory, and support facilities to accommodate 450 students. By the 2005 - 2006 school year, it became an industrial technical school that offered specialties in the areas of electricity, refrigeration, and air conditioning. A new electronics specialty was later introduced to all fourth-year students. This provided the 640-student population with training in technical and professional applications to enable entry into the labor market and the pursuit of studies at the higher education level. The institution is distinguished as the only industrial school in Vargas state that focuses on training students in specialties that are relevant to the state's employment needs. The school's socio-productive projects included working on the expansion of water filters, especially frozen water, through the use of reusable materials.

Over the years, students, teachers, and staff have been plagued by robberies, thefts, and other criminal activities. They have requested assistance from officers of the People's Guard to protect them from the crime. At some point, there was a need for permanent police presence since continuous protection was considered as the only solution that would ensure all could be safe at school. Crime plaguing the surrounding areas is an ongoing problem that has continued to affect all at the school and the learning environment.

Veroes, Yaracuy State

Veroes was officially established in 1909, but slaves were transported there to work the cocoa and sugarcane plantations during earlier years. So, the history of the region goes as far back as the colonial era. Many slaves escaped and fled to the mountains to show their resistance to servitude. These Maroons formed communities where their freedom and self-governance enabled them to unite for their cause to remain free people who could enjoy equality and co-exist as a community. They formed the communities of Agua Negra, Palmarejo, Taría, and the Jua

Jua. The communities of the runaways were known as the Black Zone of the Yaracuy State.

Veroes has been considered the most depressed region of the Yaracuy state. Up until the 1990s, the municipality had only one high school for the entire secondary school population. Despite the setbacks, residents in the community of Palmarejo and neighboring areas have been recognized for speaking Loango, a dialect that has been passed down since slavery. Palmarejo, was also acknowledged when President Chávez opened the Yolanda Estranga Community Complex that houses Radio Veroes 97.7 FM, a library, along with an information, documentation, and research center. The president also officially opened the Andresote Community Cultural Space in Palmarejo. These community centers are important for the enrichment of the Afro-Venezuelan culture.

Farriar, Veroes

Farriar, in Veroes, was founded during the 1800s under the name La Rosita (Virlarys, 2015). La Rosita was discovered by African descendant whose ancestors were captured and transported to the municipality. The descendants built their new homes in the town after moving from the nearby Agua Negra community, and they called the area, Hoya Farriar. By 1935, the town, then simply known as Farriar, became the capital of the Veroes. The farmers grew crops such as banana, cassava, yam, corn, and beans among other produces. Their diet included fish and also game that hunters caught throughout the deep forest. Chores were completed with water from the Marcano and Yaracuy rivers. Donkey and horse were the means of transportation, but most people walked to and from their destinations.

Inspired by the founding of Farriar, individuals in the town came together to form groups that would move away and start their own self-named communities. Virlarys (2015), informs, however, that the population in the Farriar continued to grow rapidly with residents relocating from Agua Negra, El Chino, and Los Canizos to avoid constant floods. Others moved from Palmarejo after a fire destroyed much of that town. The population growth encouraged an interest from the Bolivar Railway to extend the railway line to the area so as to enable transportation of merchandise such as banana and coco from coastal towns to other parts of Venezuela and their subsequent export to Europe and Caribbean islands. (Martinez & Diaz, 2014). The addition of the railway brought economic growth to the community. Besides the general use of the railway station, it also became a place for children to learn because there were no school buildings. Martinez & Diaz (2014) mention that the drop-out rate, however, was high because many children were expected to help their parents in the fields and house, carry water from the Marcano River, wash clothes in the river, search for wood to cook, and do other chores. Furthermore, children were not used to going to school, so many did not like to attend because they could not adapt to the learning environment.

Cultural activities are recognized by the residents of Farriar who participate in annual commemorations that include Tambores de San Juan Bautista, a popular religious celebration. Moreover, for over 200 years, residents engage in monthly religious celebrations in each community in honor of individual saints of the churches.

Francisco Herrera Vega High School
Liceo Abigail Lozano Educational Unit
Liceo Juan Avendaño de Farriar

As late as the 1980s, students living in Farriar, Agua Negra
and Palmarejo had to travel long distances or relocate
outside of the Veroes Municipality to continue their
education at a secondary school such Francisco Herrera
Vega High School in El Guayabo. The travelling issues
ended once Liceo Abigail Lozano Educational Unit, the
first secondary school, was opened in Farriar. The
curriculum at the secondary school includes participation in
a socio-cultural productive curriculum. This is an
educational technique that has allowed teachers working at
schools in Afro-Venezuelan communities to plan their
curriculum around the culture of their surroundings. The
program has allowed students to learn about their history,
culture, environment, economy, cuisine, alternative
medicine, and society. In so doing, students participate by
exchanging knowledge not only inside the classroom but
outside with members of the community.

Liceo Abigail Lozano received structural damages some
years shortly after its construction. As a result, major reconstruction work was undertaken to make the buildings
safe and accessible to students, teachers, and support staff.
The work included the renovation of five classrooms and
four other classrooms were demolished and re-constructed
to accommodate more than 1,080 secondary students and
those enrolled in the diversified educational program. The
work, which was completed in 2014, also included the refurbishing of other educational spaces that were
subsequently furnished entirely and equipped with
computers. Renovations were also done to the bathrooms.
Liceo Juan Avendaño de Farriar, was another Bolivarian
secondary school that was later constructed in Farriar to

accommodate more than 600 students and aid in the overcrowding at Liceo Abigail Lozano.

Barlovento, Miranda State

The Miranda State is recorded in the 2011 census as the most populated state with Afro-Venezuelans with an estimated 158,000 residents. Many of these residents live in Barlovento, a county or parish in Miranda State. Slaves were forced to work on cocoa plantations, and those who escaped formed small hidden communities or cumbes in Barlovento's mountains.

Acevedo is the largest city in Barlovento with approximately 150,000 residents. Other notable cities in Barlovento, with rapid growth, include Andrés Bello, Brión, Buroz, Páez, and Pedro Gual. Higuerote, Rio Chico, and San Jose de Barlovento are a few of the towns associated with these cities.

Barlovento is known for its agricultural production of crops such as cacao, beans, and plantains. In fact, Barlovento is recognized as one of the most important cocoa producing areas in the country. Its cocoa crops were declared cultural assets by the Institute of Cultural Heritage of Venezuela in 2005. A gigantic sculpture, known as Monument to Cacao, displays a ripe, closed cocoa pod that stands on a base in the center of a plaza in San Jose de Barlovento. The massive monument is a testament to the historical, cultural, and environmental value of cocoa to the residents of Barlovento for generations since slavery.

Barlovento is also recognized for rich history, art, and cultural celebrations of its African heritage. The combination of African and Spanish cultures is evident in the rhythmical drumming and dancing in Barlovento's

Afro-Venezuelan celebrations that include the Feast of San Juan, the Entierro de la Sardina, and Day of the Dead. The people are also known for their artisan skills in transforming wicker into baskets, sewing boxes, and other items. Also, skilled artists make a living by creating and selling embroidery, crochet, macramé, ceramics, woodwork and paper creations at the Las Mimbreras craft center and other places.

Universidad Politecnica Territorial de Barlovento Argelia Laya

It was uncommon to find a university or post-secondary institution in areas where Afro-Venezuelans were the predominant population. Then, during the 1970s, a movement of Barloventeñas and Barloventeños was formed that fought for the creation of a university for Barlovento. Distinguished professors and the community united to make the post-secondary needs of Barlovento a reality. The Windward University Institute was officially established on March 14, 1991, in Higuerote, Brion.

The university opened with an enrollment of 290 students, 17 professors, two administrative staff and two ancillary workers. Since its inception, the university's three level building has housed classrooms, administrative facilities, along with student services spaces such as a library, a student welfare office, a grocery store, and a cafeteria. The premises also include sports fields, maintenance facilities, parking and green areas. The incoming class was trained within three years in business administration, agricultural marketing, tourism and hospitality. Training was conducted in partnership with private sector-run programs which generated oversight from the government for the state subsidized funding.

The university, now known as Universidad Politecnica Territorial de Barlovent Argelia Laya (UPTBAL), uses community, environment, and social criteria for the six cities of Barlovento and their capital towns to determine the locations post-secondary courses will benefit the most. This methodology determines that civil construction courses would be most useful in the cities of Andres Bello and Pedro Gual; administration courses in the cities of Acevedo and Eulalia Buroz; computer courses in Acevedo and Paez; and agricultural courses in the Acevedo, Andres Bello, and Pedro Gual cities. Other offerings include culinary arts, nutrition, and tourism. The university's curriculum reflects regional innovative projects that require students to interact with their communities. Students engage in theory and practical projects that involve presentations, meetings, workshops, seminars, courses, conferences and other learning methods that entail research related to the development of their communities. Linking learning to the community has enabled the university to influence not only the socio-cultural geographical areas of the state but also the institution's contributions to training highly qualified professionals with skills that are needed throughout Venezuela. In turn, graduates from the university gain a sense of belonging, and they acquire a social commitment to work with local, regional, and national authorities along with their communities.

Pedagógico Instituto de Miranda
"José Manuel Siso Martínez

The Pedagogical Institute of Miranda José Manuel Siso Martínez (IPMJMSM), was established by decree in 1976, to address the need for teachers. At the time of its founding, the institution was known as the Pedagogical Institute of the East. By resolution from the Ministry of Education in 1978, its name was changed to the Experimental

Pedagogical University Institute "José Manuel Siso Martínez" in honor of the distinguished Guyanese educator. In 1988, the teachers' college became associated with the Pedagogical Experimental University of Libertador, the main public university institute for teachers and professors in Venezuela. In 1993, another name change was made to the Pedagogical Institute of Miranda "José Manuel Siso Martínez".

Since the institution's opening, efforts have been made to train teachers to meet the rising demand not only in the city or state but in other parts of the country. The main campus is located at Urbina, but Afro-Venezuelan students living along the Barlovento coast and the surrounding communities may attend the Río Chico extension in Páez. Students may choose from a wide range of academic offerings in physical education, natural sciences and mathematics, industrial technical education, human development, geography and history. They may also complete an internship at the end of the program. Secondary school teachers are trained at the teachers' college for at least five years.

Maracaibo, Zulia State

According to the 2011 census, Zulia is the second most populated state of Afro-Venezuelans with approximately 109,000 residents. The first official record of Africans in Maracaibo appears to have occurred in 1604 when a slave ship ran aground in nearby Coro, and those slaves were transported to and sold in Maracaibo (Tinker Salas, 2009). However, another report indicates slaves were also taken to the western part of Venezuela prior to that date. Although the region did not receive as many slaves as the central cocoa producing states such as Miranda, slaves appeared to have continuously been processed and sold in Maracaibo.

Reports indicate that slaves were also used as sailors aboard vessels travelling along Lake Maracaibo. Tinker Salas (2009) wrote that by the beginning of the 19th century, 3,734 slaves legally resided in Maracaibo. However, that number did not account for the much larger Zulian state's biracial population of African heritage.

Catholicism is now embraced as the primary form of worship for Afro-Venezuelans in Maracaibo. The religion is not only symbolic but is also known for bringing together the local community which creates a lasting effect (Charier, 1999). This religious association transcends into the celebration of the Fiesta of the Black Saint, San Benito, from December 26th to January 2nd. in the Afro-Venezuelan villages south of Maracaibo Lake. The popular worship of San Benito is celebrated with the playing of chimbánguele drums. Feria de la Chinita is another well-known religious festival that is celebrated annually in the city of Maracaibo.

Universidad Nacional Experimental Rafael Maria Baral

Universidad Nacional Experimental Rafael Maria Baral (UNERMB) was opened in Maracaibo for those who otherwise would not have had an opportunity to obtain a post-secondary education in Maracaibo or other areas throughout Zulia state. Planning and feasibility studies to open a university on the east coast of Lake Maracaibo began since June 1979 at the Cabimas office, and a presidential decree was issued on March 15, 1982 on the establishment intentions. On July 20th of that year, the name National Experimental University "Rafael María Baralt" (UNERMB) was selected. Work in developing the institution continued until October 24, 1983 when the university was officially opened to students.

The school initially offered industrial management courses that were attended by 120 students and taught by 15 professors. By 1984, enrollment increased when education, mathematics, and practical subjects were added. In 1985, UNERMB offered specialist and master's degree programs in higher education instruction, basic education administration, financial management, and human resources management in Cabimas, Maracaibo, and Valera in Trujillo State. Continued expansion of the university has been responsible for the opening of east coast extension campuses in Ojeda City, Los Puertos de Altagracia, and Mene Grande. Subsequent expansions enabled other extension openings in Santa Ana de Coro, Bachaquero, Santa Rita, the Bobures, and the Port of Altagracia. The university has increased its enrollment expeditiously in education, administration, health, along with engineering and technology. Post-graduate studies now include a Ph.D. degree in education.

Universidad Nacional Experimental Politécnica de la Fuerza Armada Bolivariana

Universidad Nacional Experimental Politécnica de la Fuerza Armada Bolivariana (UNEFA) is a Venezuelan public university associated with the Venezuelan Armed Forces. It was founded in 1974 as Instituto Universitario Politécnico de las Fuerzas Armadas Nacionales. Three divisions of the institution were initially created: The Army Military Engineering School that trained civil engineers; School of Communications and Electronics of the Ministry of Defense that trained electronic engineers; and the Postgraduate School of the Navy that trained mechanical and electrical engineers. All three were eventually consolidated into one institution with the primary mission of training professionals in their chosen careers entailing science or industry or technology or social sciences. The combined effort was also associated with establishing the Bolivarian National Armed Forces to support the country's military needs. The institution was renamed by President Chavez in 1999 as Universidad Nacional Experimental Politécnica de la Fuerza Armada Bolivariana (UNEFA). By 2009, the university had an enrollment of approximately 235,000 students and located in every Venezuelan state except Monagas.

Throughout the years, UNEFA Zulia has expanded its academic offering in Maracaibo with new undergraduate and graduate degrees, doctoral programs, and also career programs designed with a social purpose to engage the surrounding communities by offering them courses and workshops of interest. Courses taught at UNEFA Zulia are naval engineering, petrochemical engineering, system engineering, telecommunications engineering, municipal administration and management, disaster management, and tourism. The university continues to integrate academics and defense by maintaining an active army reserve, a military battalion prepared to defend each state, and a marching band to develop the musical talents of students.

Culture is an important aspect of the learning process at UNEFA. So, students may get involved in extra-curriculum activities that are associated with theatre, traditional and contemporary dance, music, ensembles, vocal groups, visual arts, and other creative areas. The social activities provide students with an opportunity to develop lasting friendships as they interact while learning about, organizing, and expressing their cultural talents.

El Callao, Bolivar State

The 2011 census includes an estimate of 68,000 Afro-Venezuelans in Bolivar State. El Callao became known when gold mines were discovered in that parish in 1853. The mines boosted the economy as production increased in 1885. The town became home to a large West Indian skilled labor force that migrated there to work in the mines during the late 19th century. The immigrant workers came from predominantly Trinidad, but others migrated from Dominica, Grenada, St. Lucia, St. Kitts and Nevis and to a lesser extent St. Martins and Martinique. The first gold rush ended by 1899. Many of the migrant workers remained in Venezuela after the closing. For many years, perceptions were that the mines had been depleted of its mineral. However, during the 1970s, a Venezuelan national mining corporation invested in re-vamping the industry since it could make substantial profits on the high gold prices. Another reason was that the mining company possessed modern equipment to gain easier access to the mineral. The re-opening brought employment to the descendants of those earlier migrants from the islands.

Over a century, residents have maintained the traditions of their West Indian ancestors through customs such as the celebration of carnival a week prior to the beginning of Lent. During that time, the sounds of West Indian calypso fills the air similar to earlier periods. The founder of carnival, Madama Isidora Agnes, known as Negra Isidora, is a popular re-created figure in the carnival street parade. This colorfully dressed re-curing figure appears in the form of impersonators dressed as devils or a fantasy figure. Musical instruments such as the bumbac, rallo, bell, and Venezuelan cuatro blare loudly as spectators move to the rhythm of the infectious sounds. Afro-Venezuelans not only enjoy the rhythms of the music passed down from a combination of English and French cultures, but generations have continued to speak English mixed with patois. They maintain traditions that also extend to the preparation of foods eaten centuries ago by their ancestors.

National Experimental University of Guayana

In 1979 the Corporación Venezolana de Guayana decided that it was time for a university to be established in the parish to produce trained professionals who could become knowledgeable about industrial activities in the region. They recognized a need for post-secondary educated workers to undertake jobs to support the consolidation of regional development of Guayana. The corporation also wanted students to learn extensively about the cultural and social aspects of the region. So, in accordance with a presidential decree in 1982, planning, organization, and feasibility studies began for the development of the Universidad del Sur which was later changed to National Experimental University of Guayana (UNEG).

Planning for the university included opening programs in areas such as engineering, administration, and education. Suggestions were made to introduce master's level programs along with undergraduate courses and later add doctoral programs. The headquarters of the university was expected to be located in Bolivar City where a building was already provided, but campuses were also intended in Guayana City, and Upata. The university was intended to be a regional higher education institution that would remain an independent entity that promotes research and undertakes regional causes in Guayana.

UNEG's El Callao campus was opened in 1996. The school's administration was made responsible to bear all costs to develop and maintain programs at its extension campus. Two programs were initially opened - the career projects course in administration and accounting and a bachelor's degree course in integral education. Both courses represented areas that were considered important to the demands of communities in El Callao. By 2001, the administration could no longer afford to support the financial upkeep of the programs at El Callao campus. The threat of closure of the programs caused staff and students to take their concerns to National Universities Counsel, the National Assembly, and the Legislative Assembly of the Bolivar State. UNEG now provides the resources to maintain programs on the El Callao campus. The main campus has also been responsible to oversee any difficulties related to an instability of teaching staff and any lack of adequate infrastructure at the El Callao campus. The school has expanded its offerings to include undergraduate courses in banking and finance administration, fiscal science, integrated education as well as public accounting and tourism.

Central American Journey

Central America
And Education

The Central American region is comprised of the countries of Belize, Guatemala, El Salvador, Honduras, Nicaragua, Panama, and Costa Rica. Africans were transported by Spanish colonists to Central America during the 16th and 17th centuries. The largest population of those of African descent resides predominantly in Nicaragua along the Mosquito Coast of the Caribbean Sea. Costa Rica is home to the descendants of both Afro-Costa Ricans of African descent and Afro-Antillean primarily of Jamaican heritage. In Panama, people of African descent were present prior to the construction of the Panama Canal, and that population increased with workers migrating from Caribbean countries. Honduras has a small population of Afro-Hondurans who are mainly of Garifuna heritage. Afro-Guatemalans reside mainly in the Caribbean state of Izabal, and their heritage is associated with both the Garifuna and other Afro-Caribbean people. The Black population in Central America also includes a combination of the Garifuna and Miskitu indigenous cultures. The combined Spanish and indigenous heritage of Mestizos have dominated national identity philosophies throughout Central America since the post-colonial period. This has caused African ancestry, social, and political involvement to have less prominence than the contributions of the Mestizos. Consequently, due to a lack of a sense of place and belonging, as well as genetics and cultural mixing, some people of African descent in Central America have tended to identify themselves as something other than Black.

Afro-Latinos are gradually making strides throughout Central America although they are still affected by a long history of displacement and exclusion. Therefore, they are more than likely to be categorized in groups of chronic poverty that receive fewer years of education. In El Salvador, children of African descent would be included in the approximately 50 percent number of students who stop attending school after grade 6. Same applies to those living in Guatemala, where less than 40 percent of children continue their education and begin to study at secondary schools. Furthermore, Afro-Nicaraguan children are included in the two-shift attendance system that was established to accommodate them and others who need to work during the daytime to help their families financially. In addition, Belize's schools, based on the British system, require mandatory primary school attendance, but many children have to quit school to work and support their families.

Nicaragua
Education During and After Slavery

Most slaves who were transported to Nicaragua by the
Spanish during the 16th century blended with the Mestizo
and white population from generation to generation. As a
result, their descendants gradually lost all appearances
connected with their Black ancestors. Therefore, most
Afro-Nicaraguans today are associated with slaves who
were imported by the British when they colonized the
Caribbean coastline of Nicaragua during the 17th century.
A mass migration of slaves arrived in Nicaragua from
Jamaica during the 19th century and thereafter. Later, a
group of Garifuna people from Honduras settled in the area.
For the Jamaican slaves, the British had forbidden them to
read and write so undoubtedly the ruling classes'
uncompromising stance on educating indentured laborers
would have continued when they took their slaves with
them to the Mosquito Coast of Nicaragua. However, any
freed Blacks or biracial immigrants choosing to migrate to
Nicaragua on their own may have already acquired the
ability to read and write in Jamaica and other islands. Later,
the church, especially the Moravians, appeared to have
played an important role in educating the large Black
population in Bluefields, Nicaragua. The Moravian
missionaries arrived in Bluefields around 1847 to begin
their evangelistic ministry. This group established the
Moravian Church in 1849. The church's mission, to
convert, was initially directed toward the Miskitu people.
However, most of the Black populations of Jamaican roots
not only gravitated towards the Moravian church on
Sundays but also attended prayer meetings, Sunday school,
and day school. So, these frequent meetings of the
congregation provided them with opportunities to learn to
read the bible or any other religious materials. In addition,
since education was a priority for the Moravians, teachers

were among the missionaries who migrated to the Mosquito Coast. The church showed an interest in educating the population by constructing schools adjacent to every church in communities. The first school was built during the second half of the 19th century. English was used in these schools as the primary language of instruction. The education students received at the Moravian schools enabled them to become teachers, pastors, and even middle managers during the period of U.S. economic investment in the region.

In 1894, the Nicaraguan government took control of the coastal region and opened several primary schools. In boosting their new authority over the English-speaking residents of Bluefields and the other coastal regions, the government issued a law requiring that all instructions were to be carried out in Spanish (Frazier, 2007). The state argued that the compulsory Spanish language requirement would not only bring about a linguistic change along the coast but enhance civic pride and appreciation for the Spanish style of governance in Nicaragua. The government emphasized that a teacher who taught only in English or some other language would not be able to perform the instructional duties effectively, and they could be fined or imprisoned. The government also threatened parents with fines and imprisonment for refusing to send their children to schools that provided instructions only in Spanish. According to Frazier (2007), the Spanish only laws not only affected the government primary schools, but the law eventually extended to the private religious schools that were also expected to yield to the demands of amending their age-old English speaking instructional methods and curriculum to Spanish. As a result, private institutions associated with the Moravian and Anglican churches closed their doors for over 20 years to avoid fines or face any arrest. After the closing of the private schools, the rural population experienced a high rate of illiteracy because the few public primary schools only offered one or two years of schooling.

When the private schools eventually reopened, Spanish became the official language of instruction. They joined the educational system implemented in the primary schools where Afro-Nicaraguans were forced to learn in Spanish instead of maintaining the English language learning traditions inside the classroom. Nevertheless, learning English continued to be passed down from generation to generation at homes in Bluefields and elsewhere. The government injustices lasted for approximately 80 years until 1979 when the Sandanista Revolution caused a change in teaching policies that instigated a return to teaching in the native languages of the Atlantic coastal residents and the integration of their culture into the curriculum (Migge, Leglise & Bartens, 2010)

Even today, there is a high illiteracy rate throughout the rural areas because many cannot afford to attend school. Furthermore, secondary education is still considered a luxury of which many poorer Nicaraguans can only dream of obtaining. Some students, however, are fortunate to graduate from grade 12 and further their studies at a university.

For centuries, there was no post-secondary institutions on the Caribbean coastal region, so Afro-Nicaraguan students graduating from the grade 12 in Bluefields and elsewhere throughout the coast would have to attend a university outside of the region. In 1975, the National Autonomous University of Nicaragua (UNAN) in Managua, implemented a university extension program in Bluefields and other regions to address the need for secondary school teachers in areas such as natural sciences, English, chemistry, biology, mathematics and Spanish (URACCAN website, n.d.). The programs also provided high school graduates with an opportunity to study the first year of university or complete general studies without having to leave the Caribbean coast. The downside to this effort was that courses were taught by UNAN professors who did not have in-depth knowledge of the region, so natural resources were not incorporated into the students' learning. In 1980, the extension programs were terminated due to claims from UNAN's administration of a decrease in budget to finance the extensions' upkeeps and the inability to attract professors from Managua to the coastal region (URACCAN website, n.d.). The move was disappointing to the Caribbean region especially to those students whose graduation had to be postponed. Thereafter, the government started a rotating scholarship program for coastal students who had to travel the long distance to the Pacific region to continue their studies. However, many of the academic program selections at UNAN Managua were not relevant to the Caribbean region. Some coastal students, whose degrees where more applicable to Managua based jobs, remained on the Pacific coast after graduation where they could find employment opportunities and salaries comparable to their professional training. Others also adapted further to living on the Pacific coast by marrying and acclimating to the new customs instead of re-establishing themselves in their native coastal traditions. Most of the coastal students who received scholarships, however, did not graduate for several reasons such as: the lack of financial assistance since the scholarship did not cover all the needs of students living outside their region; inability of students to adapt to the environment at a university that lacked an intercultural approach; and abandoning studies in search of employment. So, there was a great need to open a university throughout the coastal region in areas such as Bluefields.

Bluefields, South Caribbean Autonomous Region

Bluefields, a remote coastal town, was established during the early 17th century. Slaves began arriving later that century. After the British became the ruling sovereignty for that part of Nicaragua in 1740, more slaves were transported to work on the plantations in Bluefields and elsewhere. In addition, an influx of indentured laborers from Jamaica came with their British masters After the abolition of slavery in Nicaragua in 1824, Maroons who escaped from slavery in Jamaica also found a haven in Bluefields. Furthermore, many free men from Jamaica and a smaller group of migrants from other Caribbean islands made their way across the ocean to Bluefields and other towns along the Mosquito Coast. Mestizos, and Garifuna also settled in Bluefields, which later became the capital of the South Caribbean Autonomous Region (RACS) in Nicaragua. Approximately two-thirds of the Afro-Nicaraguan population still resides in and around Bluefields along the eastern coast also known as the Mosquito Coast. Afro-Antilleans from countries such as Belize reside in the Bluefields community too.

People throughout Nicaragua seem to know little and do not have a favorable impression of Afro-Nicaraguans living in Bluefields and on the Atlantic Coast (Nittle, 2017). Residents of Bluefields and elsewhere are barred entry from certain places and even schools. Everyday racism limits Afro-Nicaraguans' career opportunities. Discriminatory practices also deprive them of human dignity which includes the use of their native language in the workplace or in schools despite the law that gave Creoles the right to use their mother tongue where they desire throughout Nicaragua.

Only about one out of five residents in Nicaragua's predominantly Afro-Nicaraguan neighborhoods has access to clean water in comparison to the national average of three in five (Burch, 2007). Between 4 percent and 17 percent have electricity, as opposed to the national average of 49 percent. Although the Atlantic Coast has been settled since the 17th century, the first road connecting the coast to the rest of the country only opened during the 20th century. Nevertheless, the roads in Bluefields and the Caribbean coast remain impassable during the rainy season and do not extend all the way throughout the Caribbean coast as of this writing.

Bluefields is recognized as a cultural extension of Afro-Anglo Caribbean people since English language is spoken and the Protestant faith is the main choice of residents. Afro-Nicaraguans in Bluefields speak a variety of English called Western Caribbean Creole, a dialect closely related to Jamaican patois. Extension of culture is also evident during a week-long festival known as Mayaya. The festival takes place in Bluefields during the last week of May. Residents perform the British traditional maypole or palo de mayo dance, and they rock to the dominant rhythm of reggae music.

Moravian High School

Moravian Junior High School was founded on March 14, 1921 by the Moravian missionaries. When the Moravian church settled in Bluefields, they began providing religious and academic education to the residents. The church realized that the residents of Bluefields were entitled to more than primary school education. Since the Nicaraguan government had not placed any emphasis in constructing a secondary school, the church opened the Moravian Junior High School. The instruction was in Spanish to comply with the government's Spanish only laws. Students of the Class of 1949 were the last graduates of the Moravian Junior High School prior to its name change to Colegio Moravo. Currently, Colegio Moravo has an enrollment of approximately 750 students and 32 teachers. Many of the school's graduates are recognized in social, political, cultural and economic accomplishments throughout Nicaragua and other parts of the world.

Horatio Hodgson High School

Horatio Hodgson High School (HHHS) was opened in response to threats to the extinction of the language, history, culture, traditions, and beliefs handed down to Afro-Nicaraguan from their English-speaking descendants. The language spoken in the homes and community was not taught at school in Bluefields, so the South Atlantic Autonomous Region approved the construction of HHHS. According to Brown (Pitsch & Ritzenthaler, 2001) if you lose your language, you lose your culture. The institution opened its doors in March 1996 in Bluefields to Afro-Nicaraguan students who wanted to continue their education after graduating from the 6th grade's Bilingual Intercultural Education Program (PEBI). HHHS is located on the banks of El Gueto in the Beholdeen neighborhood and caters to approximately 225 students of which 95 percent were born in the area. The institution is known as the only high school in the region that provides bilingual intercultural education to Afro-Nicaraguan students in the South Autonomous Atlantic Region. Prior to 1996, those Afro-Nicaraguan students who wanted to continue their education had no choice but to attend a monolingual private or public secondary school in Bluefields that taught in Spanish and offered English as a second language. At the time of writing, students occupied three classrooms which have not provided adequate space for the population.

Nevertheless, students have continued to be grounded in English before they explore Spanish. The curriculum and programs at HHHS were designed by educators specifically to incorporate academics with the culture of the Afro-Nicaraguans residents in Bluefields.

The neighborhood where HHHS is located is known for its high alcohol consumption and drugs sale. Rosales (2003) reports on a conversation with Mary Ann Simmons Woo, director of the school. The director shared that her intention is to rescue the community by giving children the opportunity to attend school. Her remarks reflect that it is common to see a dysfunctional family with a parent on drugs in the community. So, HHHS provides a chance for the children to escape that environment each day. Since the school is located in a drug infested community, class instructions include an emphasis on the importance of independence, self-esteem, culture, self-identify and solutions to uplift the residents. Another issue at the school is that most available textbooks reflect the dominant Mestizos culture and say little about ethnic minorities such as Afro-Nicaraguans. One way the school deals with the problem is to have HHHS students transcribe oral histories from their parents and grandparents about families and neighborhoods. According to Brown (Pitsch & Ritzenthaler, 2001) the efforts are helping to rescue and preserve Afro-Nicaraguan culture.

HHHS receives support solely from the Ministry of Education, Culture, and Sport (MECD) which is responsible for paying the salaries of some teachers. The school is also maintained with the low monthly tuition charged to students along with funds from local and international contributors. At the time of writing, government funding had not been forthcoming in requests to build additional classrooms. The lack of attention does not prevent the school from participating and making all efforts to excel in academics, sports, and other extracurricular activities.

University of the Autonomous Regions of the Nicaraguan Caribbean Coast, Bluefields Campus

The need to create a university located along the Caribbean coast materialized in 1978 during an organizational meeting of young Caribbean coastal leaders, including the region's college graduates. The major topic centered on a desire for a regional university because Caribbean coastal people did not have access to higher education unless they travelled the long distance to western Hispanic dominated areas of Nicaragua where Spanish is the primary language. The University of the Autonomous Regions of the South Caribbean Coast (URACCAN), a public institution with its main campus in Kamla, responded to the need by opening an extension campus in Bluefield. The opening of the Bluefields Campus has signified a desire to provide post-secondary education to the marginalized Afro-Caribbean Creole and Garífuna residents living throughout the eastern half of the country. This extension campus houses the first and only state-run higher education institution for Afro-Nicaraguan students. The National Council of Universities approved the opening of the Bluefields Campus in 1992 (URACCAN website, n.d.). Legal status was granted by the National Assembly in 1993. The university was recognized by the Nicaraguan National Council of Universities in 1995, at which time, the state-operated URACCAN Bluefields opened its doors to approximately 330 students.

Students may enroll in classes for specialty subjects such as: agroforestry, engineering, fishing engineering, sociology, and business administration. The campus has a computer lab used by students enrolled in various careers especially those majoring in computer science. The extension campus facilities also include a language lab to assist students studying foreign and native languages. These and other labs provide students with the support needed to enhance their main courses.

The university receives government funding but has to compete with older, more established universities in Hispanic Nicaragua to obtain a fair share of national funding. The university is located in a poor region where tuition is extremely low to accommodate the students' financial deficiencies. As a result, a substantial amount of the university's budget goes towards student scholarships. Outside funding sources also play a great role in assisting the institution with their financial needs. For example, funds were raised at the National Conference of URACCAN alumnae and supporters in Chicago during the 1990s. Through contributions and support from European universities and organizations too, URACCAN is able to provide its students with a high standard of education.

URACCAN is committed to working with Bluefields and its surrounding communities. Efforts include the institution's use of a grant to continue the previous work of the Regional Education System to revitalize the Garifuna language and cultural traditions of exiled residents from St. Vincent during the 18th century. Moreover, up until 2017, URACCAN was instrumental in the development of an extra-curricular project to assist in the growth of inter-cultural education among boys and girls residing within and outside of Bluefields. Furthermore, the university interacts with the community by offering many outreach or short-term courses to improve the technical skills of the working population. These courses are focused on community-based and participatory initiatives to contribute to the self-empowerment of residents.

Bluefields Indian and Caribbean University

Bluefields Indian and Caribbean University (BICU) was founded by the Moravians on June 6, 1991. Its main campus is located in the city of Bluefields. This is another option for Afro-Nicaraguan students who want to continue their post-secondary education. The privately funded institution was created with the purpose of providing higher education at the technical and professional level to assist in the human resources development of residents along the Nicaraguan Caribbean coast. BICU received authorization from the National Council of Universities in 1992 and was declared the first official accredited, main campus university of the region in 1994 (BICU website, n.d.). The institution became the 23rd member of the University of the Central American University Superior Council in 2017 (Consejo Superior Universitario Centroamericano, n.d.).

In 2017 BICU had an enrollment of more than 8,000 multi-ethnic undergraduate and graduate students, and it continues to grow steadily. The faculty includes approximately 430 full and part-time professors, and 530 administrative employees complete the staff. BICU has five faculties and nine academic schools including a school of medicine. The eight extensions of the campuses mean that students throughout the South Atlantic Autonomous Region have an opportunity to obtain post-secondary education. Through research, the university does not only contribute to the history, culture, traditions, and languages of the indigenous population, but it also plays an important role by promoting, documenting, publishing, and bringing cultural awareness to the large Afro-Nicaraguan population who resides in Bluefields since the territory was occupied by the British.

In order to live up to its motto, "education is the best option for the development of the people", the university works in partnership with organizations such as UNESCO to make a difference in the community. For example, both the university and UNESCO collaborated to develop the BICU lab to contribute to the prevention of violence towards children through mentorship and education. The institution hosts community workshops such as in 2015 when it accommodated 60 at-risk youths to analyze the problems they experienced in their communities. The university shared strategies that would allow the youths to progress. A mapping workshop was also conducted at the campus in 2015 in association with UNICEF This OpenStreetMap Project brought together 30 students, young professionals, and technicians from the regional government to train on the issue of mapping. Also, in association with Vienna's University of Natural Resources and Life Sciences, BICU embarked in a scientific project at its Bluefields main campus to build a climate change observatory to serve as a local platform for research and information for a vulnerable coastal region where agriculture, fisheries, forestry, tourism, and health industries are greatly impacted by weather conditions.

Panama
Education During and After Slavery

Slaves first arrived in Panama in 1513 at a time when Panama was regarded as an important territory due to having the shortest shipping route from the Atlantic coast to the Pacific coast. African slaves were needed for various jobs on the country's bustling port. Slaves were later assigned to the grueling work of transporting goods from the port across the isthmus through thousands of miles of rugged terrain. They travelled through poor weather conditions and were often ambushed by indigenous tribes. But many slaves took advantage of their knowledge of travelling the mysterious jungles by using their familiarities of the area to escape from slavery and form sparsely populated settlements in remote areas. These escaped Cimarroneras or Maroons survived by attacking mule train caravans travelling across Panama's dense interior. Their attacks impacted trade by the 1550s and caused great financial losses to the Spanish colonizers.

In addition to slaves, Panama experienced an entry of West Indian workers from Jamaica, Barbados, Martinique, and other islands. The first influx in 1849 to 1855 was predominantly Jamaicans who came to assist in building the railroad from Panama City to Colón. Another major migration occurred in 1880 during the French's failed construction attempt of the Panama Canal. The final and massive influx occurred in 1907 at the beginning of the construction of the Panama Canal, which was successfully overseen by the Americans.

Over 20,000 West Indian workers remained after the completion of the Panama Canal. However, in 1926, the xenophobia among the Panamanian government resulted in the passing of laws decreasing immigration from the West

Indies and later barring non-Spanish speaking people of African descent from entering the country. The descendants of slaves became known as Afro-Coloniales while the descendants of West Indian immigrants were recognized as Afro-Antilleans.

West Indian children, whose parents immigrated to Panama to build the railroad during the late 19th century, were not allowed to attend government schools. These children attended small schools opened by teachers who migrated largely from Jamaica. Teachers taught primary level classes in churches, homes, or elsewhere. Christ Church Academy, also known as La Academia de la Iglesia Cristiana, was opened in Colón in 1893 as the first private, full-fledged school for the children of West Indians immigrants. The Episcopalian school was fondly known in the community as Mr. Blake's School for many years until 1986 when the name was changed to Colegio Episcopal de Cristo.

Years later, during the arrival of workers and their children from the West Indies for the construction of the Panama Canal, immigrants still could not enroll in government schools. The Canal Zone did not have an organized school system either, so children of zone workers attended small private schools established earlier by the previous group of West Indian immigrants. In 1905, Culebra Silver School opened as the first Silver Roll school for children of West Indian migrants living in the Canal Zone. West Indian teachers became involved in the founding of this and other Silver Roll schools in the Canal Zone. Yet, these schools were managed by an American superintendent.

Teachers also worked with parents to achieve a high rate of literacy among the West Indian population living in the zone. However, in spite of learning accomplishments, both teachers and parents eventually realized that under the

American leadership at the zone, all intentions were for the Silver Roll educational system to serve as a method of controlling the rapidly growing West Indian immigrant population. Consequently, the Silver Roll educational system's false portrayal of serving West Indian children turned into a racial, restricted system that introduced students to a constrained educational structure that diminished students' self-worth. Problems included white school administrators giving false impression that the West Indian children enrolled in Silver Roll schools were not intellectually competent. The repressive learning environment in the Canal Zone caused some West Indian teachers to quit that school system and relocate to other growing West Indian communities in Colón or in Panama City under Panamanian government jurisdictions. Some parents withdrew their children and sent them to small private schools in Colón and Panama City where there were more learning opportunities for West Indian children than what was offered in the Canal Zone.

In 1921, St. Vincent School, the first public primary school, was opened for West Indian children in the Canal Zone area of Calidonia. However, by the end of the 1920s, West Indian children were often still not accepted into other public schools throughout Panama City and elsewhere. This discriminatory practice included the vocal outcries of Spanish-speaking teachers who made known their dissatisfaction with teaching English speaking West Indian children. Such infamous, reprehensible reaction caused the West Indian communities to continue to send children to their own English-speaking private schools to address the urgent need to school their children. Others selected the next option of sending their children to their native countries in care of a family member or friend so that their education would not be compromised as it was in the zone. Opportunities, though, existed for those Afro-Antilleans born to West Indian parents before 1928 since they had the option as Panamanian citizens to attend Panamanian public schools throughout the country. But, most parents rejected this option of sending their children to the overcrowded public schools where students ended their education at 14 years old - a young age when males were destined to take menial jobs at the canal and females were expected to perform domestic work or get married.

By the 1930s, the increasing population of workers' children in the Canal Zone did not cause the government a sense of urgency to expand education by opening secondary schools. Their attention to the problem only materialized ten years later on the opening of three public secondary schools. Colegio Abel Bravo became the oldest government secondary school that was opened in the Canal Zone in 1942, approximately a century after West Indian immigrants arrived to build Panama's railroad. Rainbow City High School and Paraiso High School were constructed thereafter. Today, Colegio Abel Bravo is the only remaining institution since the others were closed when the Canal Zone reverted to the Republic of Panama in 1979 in compliance with the treaty signed with the United States. The curriculum for those three secondary schools included science, mathematics, literature, and sports. Extra-curricular subjects such as dance, the arts, and languages were not always available as they were at the Canal Zone schools for expatriate American children. Many attending one of the three noted secondary high schools became teachers and progressive leaders who impacted the lives of younger Afro-Antilleans thereby enabling that generation to strive to be competitive and empower themselves into becoming successful Panamanians.

Up until the 1960s, many children living in predominantly West Indian communities such as Bocas del Toro attended

English-language private schools taught by Methodist teachers from Jamaica. When these English language schools closed, descendants received their formal education in Spanish only. But, many of these children often start kindergarten with little or no knowledge of Spanish since Panamanian Creole English continues to be spoken in homes as their first language.

Afro-Coloniales, descendants of slaves, residing in the remote areas, do not receive the high standard of education as Afro-Panamanian students living in the cities. Students living in the deep country areas also have to contend with the difficulty of finding teachers who are not only committed to the needs of learners in remote areas but will work in an underfunded classroom environment. Challenges have also included finding sufficient teachers to educate children of different ages and learning levels in the same classroom. While the quality of teaching staff has seen some improvement during later years, academic offerings still need to be brought up to high standards. Another issue in rural areas is that students often walk long and even treacherous distances to attend school. Furthermore, during rainy seasons, some may stop attending school because the overflow of dangerous rivers blocks their paths to school. Others have to contend with their parents pulling them out of school so they can work to help the family.

Portobelo, Costa Abajo - Colon Province

Portobelo is a small, seaside town located on the Caribbean coast of Panama. Slaves once congregated at its customs house on their arrival to work on the Atlantic coast or to be send onward to the Pacific coast. During the Spanish colonial era, Portobelo was a vibrant, bustling trading town with a successful economy. However, the town gradually began to decline and is now impoverished with run-down buildings. Portobelo's economy is reliant on tourism. Visitors tour ruins and learn about the town's Spanish colonialism and African resistance. In April, tourists flock to the town's annual Congo Afro-Coloniales carnival which benefits the economy. Visitors are attracted to rituals such as the Congo dance, songs, drumming, food, and other customs. Other main attractions for tourists are Portobelo's natural beaches, colonial forts, and the Afro-Latino El Nazareno, popularly known as the Black Christ festival that takes place in October. These customs represent the invaluable contributions, survival, and preservation of the Afro-Coloniales population from slavery until today. But even more irreplaceable is the lively Afro-Coloniales population who bring charm to the town. So, their cultural practices continue to distinguish them from Afro-Antillean.

Instituto Profesional y Tecnico Jacoba Urriola Solís

After centuries of waiting for a secondary school in Portobelo, the Ministry of Education opened Instituto Profesional y Tecnico Jacoba Urriola Solís, also known as IPT Jacoba Urriola Solis. The school is on the vocational track or cycle 1 system that offers professional or technical courses aimed to give students the technical skills needed for employment after graduation. The institution is considered a junior secondary school where students will attend between the ages of 12 to 15 years old. Although these students have to leave school at a young age, they are equipped with workings skills, unlike their parents and other Afro-Coloniales descendants who could not extend their education past the age of 12 years old. As the sole secondary school in town, its students participate in agricultural programs and academic subjects at the school. Students also engage in projects with organizations. For instance, they collaborated with the staff of Colón's

Tourism Authority of Panama (ATP) and the Municipality of Portobelo to clean up the town by removing glass, bottles, plastic, and other garbage. Students also participated in the first workshop for the adolescent population on strengthening and preventing HIV/AIDS. Additional outside efforts of students included the presentation of their wood carvings that demonstrated classroom learning of how to use natural products as a survival tool. Furthermore, students in the agricultural science class planted seedlings donated by an agricultural company and pledged with their teacher to take care of the growth of the plants.

The school has experienced its share of publicity outside of the learning arena. For instance, teachers and students demonstrated against poor building maintenance practices, deplorable facilities, teacher financial insecurities, and the need to appoint accounting and agricultural teachers. Demonstrators left the premises and took to the streets thereby closing down the main road for hours. Their protests were similar to those students at other rural schools that had been neglected by the Ministry of Education whose priorities seemed to focus instead on city schools. But, the most bizarre occurrence during the school's fairly short existence was the incident with 16 students who were mysteriously stricken by fainting spells and strange verbal noises. The community surmised that the students were possessed by unknown forces associated with a teacher's witchcraft rather than taking the word of a Catholic priest who denied that reasoning.

Palmas Bellas, Costa Abajo - Colón Province

Palmas Bellas is a town in the district of Chagres in the province of Colón with a large Afro-Coloniales population. It is divided into five sectors: Jamaiquita, Guachapali,

Pueblo Nuevo "La Loma", Mateo, and the sector of the Zone or El Pueblo. The town includes a health center, a primary school, and Colegio Anastacia Miter. Palmas Bellas is regarded as a sleepy destination that would be suited for those people who want total relaxation. But there are concerns with the eroding environment. Although the extraction of sand on the surface was prohibited by an executive resolution on January 3rd, 1996, the extraction of underwater sand was not included in the law. So, in 2005, one company left a huge gap in the soil with their extraction of underwater sand thereby causing the sea to invade residences. Slack governmental oversight was cited in granting and controlling the concessions of permits for the extraction of sand, stone, and quarry materials used for the construction industry.

Colegio Anastasia Miter

Colegio Anastasia Miter was the first secondary school in Palmas Bellas. Prior to that time, no efforts were made by the Ministry of Education to introduce secondary education to the community. Due to the secondary educational needs of children in the community, the residents decided to take action and struggled to open their own secondary school at the Palma Bella Primary School during the evening hours. It opened with 60 students and seven teachers without the endorsement of the Ministry of Education. Funding for salaries was requested and secured from the Colón Free Zone. Thereafter, the coffee bank came on board to purchase farmland and cattle for the school. In addition, the government-backed agricultural reform donated 50 acres of land for farming. When the Ministry of Education came onboard and officially opened the school in 1973, it was known as the José Pablo Paredes School. Enrollment increased to 90 students. The institution was later re-named after its first director, Anastasia Miter. At that time, the school continued to be housed at the Palmas Bellas Primary School, so students, the teaching staff, administrators, and members of the community joined forces and initiated educational projects to raise funds for the construction of a school building that was opened in 1975.

The curriculum includes farming of yucca, papayas, bananas, pigeon peas, and also rearing pigs. In addition to agricultural classes, other courses in the curriculum include Spanish language, religion, math, geography, history, natural science, industrial arts, music, and physical education. The student population are not only the ones living in the Palmas Bellas community, but also those who commute from towns such as Achote, Piña, Punta del Medio, Chagres, Salud and Icacal.

By 2013, the building and its facilities had deteriorated significantly. Problems included a crumbling latrine, poor water system, and leaking ceilings. Parents also expressed concerns on the lack of the school's academic progress and that the first cycle system was insufficient for their children's educational development. By 2015, the Ministry of Education had not responded to the concerns, so students left school to protest the poor state of the facilities. The student protest caused the Lagarto River Bridge, the only access to the area, to be closed. The 500 students from Palmas Bellas and the surrounding remote communities unleashed their frustrations by demonstrating to the rhythm of Congo music, chanting slogans, and burning tires. The protest lasted for five hours until authorities from the Ministry of Education arrived. The school's maintenance and educational concerns were simply forgotten by the ministry due to the institution's rural location. The ministry's irresponsible treatment had been prevalent not only at Colegio Anastasia Miter but other Panamanian rural schools that were simply never considered when providing funding to maintain school facilities.

Colón, Colón Province

During the Spanish colonial period, the Colón region of Panama was the center of trade, commerce, and the main town for economic development. Some African slaves who were captured and sent to this area, worked on the docks. They loaded goods onto ships that were destined for other Spanish colonies. Since the 19th century, beginning as early as the 1840s, West Indians immigrated to Panama to assist in building the Panama Railway and the Panama Canal. Many of the West Indians, especially from Jamaica and Barbados, settled in Colón between 1880 and 1920 to build the Panama Canal. Music and cultural activities were part of the popular outdoor recreation. At bars, live music was part of the night life.

During the early 20th century, Colón flourished with the construction of the canal. Residents kept well-maintained homes with manicured lawns. They attended theatres, clubs, and restaurants. Today, most Afro-Antillean descendants have continued to reside in Colón. The city now boasts a busy shipping port, a costly cruise ship terminal, a duty-free trade zone, and a gateway to the Panama Canal. However, away from these developments is a crowded Colón with an estimated population of 220,000. These residents face high unemployment; dirty streets; dilapidated colonial buildings with peeling paint; weeds growing out of some upper floors; sewage running on streets and alleyways; garbage piled up; rampant crime and despair. The reduction and ultimate closing of the American military base and transfer of the canal to Panama in 1999 accelerated Colón's steady decline (Archibold, 2013). In contrast, 40 miles away, on the other side of the

Panama Canal, Panama City progresses with new skyscrapers, the first subway in Central America, expensive malls, and restaurants. Many in Colón of African descent have resigned themselves to the fact that life in their city represents a racial divide as compared to the majority white residents living in the prosperous Panama City. As a result, many unemployed in Colón resist any consideration of relocating to find work in Panama City because of the expected racial discrimination in a city where it is prevalent against people of color.

Abel Bravo Colegio

Abel Bravo Colegio, the first public secondary school in Colón, was an alternative to the lack of high schools for the West Indian population living in the province of Colón. Prior to the school's founding in 1942, parents could not afford to enroll their children in the two private secondary schools in Colón. Abel Bravo Colegio opened as a junior high school. Fondly known as "the college", the school provided students with a sense of belonging and place where they could continue their education. Initially, the school included two major departments – an academic and a vocational division. Faculty and administration, however, remained as one body instead of separate entities for both departments. The original student body included 250 students with approximately ten teachers. Eleven students in commercial studies were among the first graduating class of 1948.

Today, approximately 2,278 students are enrolled with 120 teachers and 52 administrative staff. Within five years of the school's inception, two wings were added to provide the needed workshops, library, and gymnasium.
Throughout the years, additional construction projects have been completed to accommodate the growing student

population. The infrastructure includes ten classrooms for the seventh grade, ten classrooms for the eighth grade, and ten classrooms for the ninth grade, in addition to a support classroom. The curriculum includes the sciences, humanities, and computer science along with sports, culture, and artistic disciplines. Other secondary schools opened in Colón, but Abel Bravo continues to be recognized as the foundation that made it possible for West Indian immigrants, their future generations, and other Hispanic citizens of the Atlantic Coast to continue to learn so that they too would qualify for higher education and employment opportunities.

Universidad de Panamá
Centro Regional Universitario de Colón

University of Panama, one of the early established universities, was opened in 1935 and became the only full-fledged university in Panama for the next 30 years. No universities opened in any predominantly Afro-Panamanian community until August 2nd, 1957, when the University of Panama agreed to establish a campus at Colón's Republic of Uruguay Primary School. In 1958, Afro-Coloniales eagerly welcomed the start of Saturday classes since they no longer had to travel long distance to Panama City if they wanted to continue their education. In-spite of the negative reasoning by some cynics in Panama City to close the extension, new courses were added while the university worked to meet the increased enrollment of students in Colón. By 1960, the extension became known as Regional University Center of Columbus. The institution began to serve the continuing education needs of students graduating from secondary schools such as Colegio Abel Bravo School, Colegio José Guardia Vega, and Instituto Rufo A. Garay. By 1979, the university became known as the Regional University Center of Colón with an enrollment of approximately 1,200 students. As a full-fledged university, proper facilities were constantly sought to meet the rapid growth of students. The school was finally housed in Colón's Arco Iris where the Rainbow High School was once located. Funds were released by the government to renovate existing structures and build modern facilities. Refurbishing and new construction continue today as the needs arise to improve the premise.

The university offers bachelor's and master's degree courses in public administration, business administration, accounting, fine arts, education, natural sciences, technology, nursing, pharmacy, psychology, electronics, communications, and information technology. In 2000, the study of Afro-Panamanian culture was introduced. At the university's Institute of Traditional Ethnic and Cultural Studies, research-based studies have been conducted on the cultures of the Afro-Coloniales and Afro-Antilleans.

Rio Abajo, Panama City - Panamá Province

From 1925 to 1932, the West Indian laborers established popular movements to address severe housing shortages in some sectors of Panama City. This led many to relocate to the vast open space of Rio Abajo. Rio Abajo, named after the river flowing through its neighborhood, was first occupied with Jamaicans and Barbadians. They found it important to empower themselves by purchasing land in the area from prominent Panamanian families. Ownership of land demonstrated their ability to overcome the struggles for recognition of their rights as workers and legitimate residents and citizens of the Republic of Panama. The West Indians finally obtained approval in 1937 for Rio Abajo to be upgraded from a village to a district sub-division after a failed attempt in 1933. The upgraded status enabled the widening of the main highway along with the opening of community and educational facilities.

Rio Abajo was known for its quaint two-story wooden apartments especially in popular vicinities of La Boca Town, Diablo Heights and 19th Street. These buildings were crowded with residents who were supported by family members working at the Canal Zone. From the 1950s to the 1960s the population had started to decline with many migrating to New York for a better life. Others left later due to the high crime rate. The remaining residents continued to make Rio Abajo their home. With their love for music, they continued to participate in outdoor entertainment events, Residents also continued to meet in enclosed venues for music competitions and concerts, spent nightlife at bars or theatres, and attended reggae parties during the 1970s. In this close-knit community during earlier years, some Caribbean descendants maintained their unique culture of speaking English, but now many have assimilated into speaking Spanish only.

Over the years, many of the wooden structures have burned down or deteriorated or have been demolished. The lands have been subsequently sold to investors for construction of commercial buildings to house various industries. But, the Ministry of Housing continues to ensure that the percentage of residences for this approximately 28,000 population will remain above the rate of commercial occupancy of the land in this sub-division. Restoration of the parks and other projects have been ongoing in order to bring back hope to residents of a community that has also seen a decrease in crime.

Instituto José Dolores Moscote

The Instituto José Dolores Moscote was opened in Rio Abajo in 1956 to address the growth of students who needed secondary education. The school started in a building that previously housed the Isabel Herrera de Obaldía Professional School, but the structure was not adequately maintained throughout the years. After moving into this old building, the deplorable conditions encouraged parents and the Association of Teachers to join forces to locate new facilities that would provide a better learning environment. Their determination resulted in the government making a commitment to purchase the Convent of the Visitation building which was constructed in 1958. However, this facility too did not meet high standards to accommodate students. The frustrations from unacceptable learning conditions caused educators and parents to demonstrate. The disruption resulted in the government allocating funds for new building construction at the site where the school is presently located. Situated in the heart of Panama City, in the Lefevre Park Township, the school continues to address the growing educational needs of students who reside throughout the community.

The Instituto José Dolores Moscote is now recognized as one of the most prestigious Panamanian schools and also for its academic excellence. The 3,000-student population attend school on a morning and evening shift system. The school houses 48 classrooms, computer audiovisual labs, along with physics, chemistry, and natural sciences labs. The school's hall of music is a testament to so many who have performed with the school's musical band. The band not only plays throughout Panama, but it also has performed in other countries, such as in the United States at a Panamanian Day celebration. Students may also participate in many other extra-curriculum activities that are offered on campus.

Almirante, Bocas Del Toro Province

Another region of Panama that has a large Afro-Antillean population of West Indian background is in the northwestern province of Bocas del Toro. Bocas del Toro is located on the Caribbean coast just south of Costa Rica. The province includes the Bocas del Toro Archipelago, Almirante Bay, Chiriqui Lagoon, and adjacent mainland. The capital is the city of Bocas on Isla Colón. Other major cities or towns include Almirante and Changuinola. In the 1820s, several British planters from San Andres and Providence Islands moved with their slaves to Bocas del Toro which was under Colombian rule at that time. The settlement in Bocas del Toro remained small, surviving on fishing, slash-and-burn agriculture, and other basic jobs. Cacao and abaca became the main crops. After a more resistant strain of banana was introduced, that crop replaced cacao and abaca thereby making Bocas del Toro the region's most profitable banana producing area once again.

The United Fruit Company introduced bananas at the turn of the century. Similar to their actions in Costa Rica, Nicaragua, and Honduras, the company recruited Jamaicans in large numbers to work on the United Fruit plantations. During the 1940s and 1950s, disease virtually wiped out the banana plantations. Some West Indian families capitalized on the disaster and bought parcels of land on former plantations when the banana boom ended. They established small and medium sized family farms where they acquired fortunes. This led to the development of an Afro-Antillean rural middle-class community in the banana zones. The upward societal progress made them quite different from Afro-Panamanians elsewhere. In fact, this Atlantic zone is known as one of the few places in the world where bourgeois Afro-Antilleans reside.

In addition to the town of Bocas, Almirante has a large Afro-Antillean population of West Indian descendant. Almirante's first settlers were mainly descendants from Jamaica and the Lesser Antilles. They moved inland to work on the banana plantations during the early 1900s. Modern houses and structures built from blocks may be seen throughout Almirante. But many low-income residents reside in wooden houses including those once owned by the Chiquita Banana Company and sold to former employees prior to closing the plant. These houses are located on stilts over the murky, larvae infested, polluted Almirante Bay. The residences are dilapidated with rusted roofs and broken windows with no mosquito screens. Garbage infestation leaves the residents open to contracting infectious diseases. In other parts of Almirante, it is common to see garbage piled in high bundles due to the government's failures to provide garbage trucks to pick up, transport, and dispose of rubbish to a facility outside the city. Consequently, at the height of the rainy season, garbage piles mix with standing water. Some residents take charge of the situation by burning and burying their garbage to deal with the government's failures.

Despite issues, Almirante serves as a port for exporting banana. The town is also the mainland port for the 30-minute ferry or water taxi ride across the bay to Bocas. Tourist will pass through the sleepy town primarily to catch the water taxi.

Colegio Secundario de Almirante

Colegio Secundario de Almirante opened in 1978. The school began with three classrooms and 105 students who participated in the first school graduation in 1980. It served as a feeder school for the primary school leavers. During those early years, the focus was teaching commercial subjects to provide students with skills in areas such as cabinetmaking, construction, dressmaking, and electricity. Today, the curriculum has expanded with science and technology courses to meet the needs of the student population.

From the school's inception, the student population began to increase every year, and this caused a need to utilize the pavilions for classrooms. Since the existing buildings could no longer accommodate the growing population, and attendance was affected by high tides and flood rains, new premises were needed. Construction of the new facilities began in 1987 and the new infrastructure was opened in 1988.

Universidad Tecnológica de Panamá (UTP)

The College of Engineering of the University of Panama was established during the early 1970s in Panama City. In 1973, the college expanded by offering other academic programs and became known as the Polytechnic Institute in 1975. By 1981, the institution was granted legal status and Universidad Tecnológica de Panamá (UTP or La Tecnológica) was established. Other extension campuses were subsequently opened throughout Panama including one in the Bocas del Toro Province.

UTP's first extension campus in Bocas del Toro was opened on Isla Colón in June 1979 when the university was known as Polytechnic Institute. However, in 1983, the Isla Colón campus was closed due to low enrollment. This facility became the regional administrative headquarters of the university where work included promoting the university throughout various provinces including Bocas del Toro. An active promotion venture of the university led to a demand for post-secondary education to return to Bocas Del Toro province. With the urging of residents, post-secondary education was re-introduced with another extension campus in the Bocas del Toro Province. The building was constructed in the region's Changuinola municipality. Construction began in 1983, and in 1986, the campus was opened with seven classrooms and a room for professors. The second construction phase of the university began in 1991 with inauguration of new facilities in 1992. The engineering technician class with specialization in programming and analysis was opened for enrollment in 1992. The first class for postgraduate studies in senior management was offered in 1995. The inaugural class for the bachelor's degree in engineering was started in 1998. A master's degree in computer systems education began in 2006. These are only some of the many programs that are offered to students. The university has a highly selective admissions process that is not only based on entrance examination results, but all applicants must provide their academic records and secondary school class grades for consideration.

Costa Rica
Education During and After Slavery

The first Africans that arrived in Costa Rica came with the Spanish conquistadors. They worked on farms in the Atlantic region that was isolated from the rest of the country. Many worked independent of their plantation owners who only went to oversee the crops once a year. Intermixing of races occurred between Africans and the indigenous people. It was also common for Africans to cohabitate with the Spanish population. This meant that bi-racial children were freed from slavery by their white fathers. Acceptance into the Spanish culture allowed the biracial population to assimilate easily into the Costa Rican society and later in the public-school system. But, miscegenation throughout those early years meant that by the next century Blacks lost the visual identity of their African ancestors thereby making them less distinguishable from the white or indigenous populations. So, traces of a Black population were no longer evident.

The second wave of Blacks who arrived in Costa Rica occurred when Jamaicans migrated to the country in response to the United Fruit Company's (UFCO) hiring of workers in the banana industry (Castillo Serrano, 2002). Government schools were opened for the children of these Jamaican migrants. However, Afro-Caribbean parents resisted sending their English-speaking children to the public schools because they would have to learn Spanish as their first language. Furthermore, parents felt that their children would be exposed to white children who they considered less hygienic. As a result, English non-denominational schools were started throughout the Limón Province during the late 1890s to early 1900.

In the case of the denominational schools, the Baptist missionary brought their first teacher to Cahuita, Talamanca in 1905. A school sponsored by the Methodist Church in El Cairo opened its doors in 1912. Opening English schools eventually became a popular venture because almost all church denominations opened their own English schools during the 1930s and 1940s. Individual teachers and organizations such as the Universal Negro Improvement Association (UNIA) were also involved in setting up school in Costa Rica.

Students were accommodated at different learning sites. Some attended school in newly constructed wooden-frame buildings associated with churches that also served as sites for church activities. Others completed classes in often old, wooden, rented buildings. Students attending schools with minimum enrollment were taught in one room or even a corridor of a teacher's house. They were popularly known as corridor schools.

The number of enrolled students depended on various factors such as the population of a community; the number of English schools opened; the space availability; and the popularity of the teachers (Castillo Serrano, 2002). The Anglican Church schools enrolled between 150 to 200 children because their teachers were well-trained, and their buildings had enough space. The home schools, however, were constricted in their intake of students due to space limitation.

Afro-Caribbean parents sent their children to schools year-round, Monday to Friday, from morning until afternoon. Schools did not turn away any students regardless of their race, gender, or even age. Schools also did not turn away students whose parents could not afford to pay the weekly fee. According to Castillo Serrano, (2002) parents paid fees at a graded level. For instance, parents paid 25¢ for beginning students; 50¢ for the next level; 75¢ for the next level and so on. Most workers at UFCO could afford the school fees. However, those who did not work at UFCO and others who experienced difficulties with paying school fees would send a note to their child's teacher requesting an extension for the payment period. UFCO and the church helped the community by providing financial and other support to some of the schools. This grant was beneficial to those who relied on the community for school fees and other necessary items.

The curriculum of the English schools in Limón replicated the curriculum in the British colonies, specifically Jamaica. In addition to religious studies on Fridays, the curriculum followed step-by-step lessons in the English textbooks from Jamaica on subject matter including British history and geography, literature, and science plus information on Caribbean islands. Teachers enhanced the curriculum with other topics. The learning process was based on memorization, so students were expected to remember not only the multiplication tables but also meanings of words, spelling, poems, and psalms (Castillo Serrano, 2002).

In addition to classwork, private schools organized extracurricular activities and fundraising events. These activities were fun for both students and parents because they served as recreational options for the family. Students would, with the help of their teacher, prepare a play or a recitation, or a musical to entertain an audience. The performances replaced the void of not having theatres or cinemas in Limón. In addition, churches capitalized on their associated schools by using student rallies and academic contests as fund raising events.

Teachers punished students who did not complete their homework or who misbehaved in the classroom. They used a belt to enforce punishment. Teachers had such strength and power that they punished with the approval of parents. So, during that era, teachers were influential not only in their students' learning but in their students' conduct. The school was considered a continuation of students' home life and vice versa. When parents learned that their children were punished in school, they would also be punished by parents when they arrived home. Corporal punishment was eliminated during the 1960s when the private schools began to adopt the American standards of non-physical alternatives.

A small number of English schools arranged for students to hold graduation ceremonies after completing the 6th grade, and students celebrated in style. However, many institutions did not hold graduation ceremonies or even hand out diplomas to their students. The only reward those students had to look forward to after 6th grade was getting a job or continuing their education to 8th grade. After leaving school at 6th grade, the main interest of Afro-Caribbean students in Costa Rica was to obtain clerical and lower management level jobs at either the railroad or the banana industries but not in agriculture (Castillo Serrano, 2002). While their parents migrated from Jamaica with agricultural skills, the children's intentions were to avoid the hardships of working in the fields. Some thought it was beneficial to remain in school and complete the 8th grade because they would be considered an outstanding student. Such students would receive a letter of recommendation for certain jobs at the banana or railroad industries with the potential for growth.

Teacher certification standards were not required to teach in the English curriculum schools. Consequently, some teachers migrating from Jamaica were certified while others who received a basic education used that basic knowledge in the classroom. Certified or not, teachers were entrusted with a great deal of responsibility but did not reap the fruits of their labor. According to Castillo Serrano (2002), those who taught at denominational schools were not paid by the church. Instead, they obtained their salary from student fees. These fees were, in some cases, shared by schools with churches as offerings on behalf of parishioners. Nonetheless, salary limitations did not deter teachers from their commitment to maintain operations at their schools. Residents often questioned how some of these schools remained open with such financial challenges. Many did so by relying on charity from the community.

Nowadays, several secondary schools in the Limón Province have maintained high academic standards and provide their students with top notch facilities. But, for the most part, the majority of public schools on and around the Limón Province do not have good reputations (Puerto Viejo Satellite, n.d.). The quality of education is perceived as low standards because of over-crowded classes, poorly maintained facilities, short schooldays, minimal homework, and high drop-out rates. These factors create an academic gap that would require private tutoring for those affected students who want to attend university.

Limón, Limón Province

Limón was founded during the mid-1800s. Construction of the railroad created an influx of Jamaicans and Chinese laborers to the town in 1867 when work began to connect Limón to San José, the capital and largest city in Costa Rica. A second wave of Jamaican migrants arrived in the city by 1909 when the United Fruit Company (UFCO) recruited these English speakers to work in different positions throughout the banana industry.

Limón, the capital city of the Limón Province, is the center of the province's economy. The city is boosted by the location of one of the most important harbors in Costa Rica. The Atlantic location of the port enables the export of containers loaded with coffee, pineapples, and bananas. Limón also serves as the entry point for imported goods from all over the world. Furthermore, Limón is a principle port stop for major cruise ships.

When construction of the railroad was completed and after the UFCO closed its Limón operations and relocated the plant to San José, many Jamaicans and other immigrants returned to their native countries. But, a number of those unemployed immigrants remained and settled permanently in the town of Limón. They and others who remained throughout Limón Province faced government enforced apartheid tactics that restricted their movements outside of the province to seek employment until the 1948 regime change. This racist injustice instigated unemployment, poverty, and linguistic differences that still exist generations later in Limón in spite of Afro-Costa Ricans' integration into the mainstream. So, despite the ongoing lucrative port ventures in Limón, problems continue to greatly impact more than 5,000 households where residents are unable to meet at least one basic need such as clean water, sanitation, or an adequate diet.

Many of descendants of Jamaican immigrants have continued to make the Limón Province their home. The region is known as the Black Province where language is influenced by the Jamaican British dialect or Creole English. Limón Province is also considered the most multiracial province in Costa Rica. Approximately 350,000 or 8 percent of the population of Limón Province are Afro-

Costa Ricans. An estimated 240,000 of those are Afro-Antillean with Jamaican heritage and at least 80,000 reside in the capital town of Limón. About 33 percent of bi-racial residents of identifiable African descent also reside in Limón Province. An estimated 50,000 Afro-Antilleans live in San José, and others are scattered elsewhere outside of the Limón Province.

Limón is known for the annual carnival celebrations of its Afro-Caribbean culture during October. Throughout the entire week, beginning at 5:00 A.M. each day, bands of local musicians, known as Cimarrona, march through the streets with their percussion and wind instruments. The loud noises awake residents, alerting them that a new day has dawned, and it is time for the celebrations to begin. Sounds of British Caribbean calypso and reggae music dominate sounds in the streets of Limón. Marching bands, drummers, and dancers parade day and night through the city. The inviting aroma of food fills the air with the smell of rice and beans, jerk chicken, rondon, coconut shrimp, meat patties, and pan bon cake. The Grand Parade, on the final day of celebrations, is the culmination of the festivities.

Another reminder of history and culture in Limón was the Black Star Line Inc. premises, the oldest building in the city. The Black Star Line Inc. was founded by the Jamaican activist Marcus Garvey. The organization's building in Limón was constructed in 1922. This structure was the town's finest example of Victorian Caribbean architecture prior to its partial destruction by fire in 2016.

Colegio Diurno de Limón

The Afro-Costa Rican population and other ethnic groups welcomed the opening of a public secondary school, The

Day College of Limón, on December 25th, 1945. At that time, the school occupied temporary facilities in the building of the former Tomás Guardia Gutiérrez School. One of the rooms was turned into a library that was under the same administration as Limón's municipal and public libraries. In 1957, the growth of the student population and the need to expand its facilities resulted in the construction of new buildings at its current location. Construction was completed and the new school doors were opened in 1959, and the official inauguration was in 1961. It was later renamed Colegio Diurno de Limón.

The Special Education Department was started at the school in response to the request of parents with disabled children. In 1995, a pilot pre-vocational program for secondary school level was introduced for students with special needs. By 2008, special needs students were integrated into regular classrooms.

Colegio Diurno de Limón presently serves a student population of approximately 1,700. Since the opening of the school, students still wear the shield with the school's motto on the left sleeve of their shirts and blouses. "Believe, create, grow" is the school's motto which is inscribed on the top of the institution's shield. The shield depicts an open book that represents the source of knowledge; an arrow points the way to wisdom that is symbolized by a star; and the shield is bordered by two laurel branches representing triumph. These symbols are associated with the lyrics of the school anthem. The shield also symbolizes that there is no difference in a student's ethnicity or religion because the school honors multi-cultural ethnicities and diverse values throughout the province. The school faced plagiarism issues when its age-old motto became commercialized as a slogan during a political campaign.

A donation from the Mixed Institute of Social Assistance (IMAS) to the school was anticipated to be used to remodel the institution's assembly hall and furnish it with equipment. Renovation was necessary because the auditorium's deteriorating infrastructure failed to meet security and building codes expected for its occupants. At the time of writing, repairs had not been started. However, expectations for repairs to the auditorium included: the stage, ceiling, and floor structure. Electrical installation and construction of walls for changing rooms were also anticipated. The renovations were not only to benefit the student population but also the assembly hall serves as an auditorium for the Limón community's cultural and social activities. Furthermore, the auditorium serves 500 students from the Avancemos program that caters to those who show a high risk of dropping out of school due to economic and other reasons.

University of Costa Rica – Caribbean Headquarters

Since the 1960s, the residents of Limón had been discussing a need to open a public university. In 1975, the University Council agreed to open an extension of the University of Costa Rica (UCR) in Limón, centuries after UCR was established in 1843. The extension campus in Limón was initially known as the Decentralized Limón Service and was under the administration of the Regional Headquarters of Turrialba. It was not easy to recruit highly qualified professors, obtain necessary educational resources, or even secure an adequate location to hold classes. So, only general studies and some basic or required courses were offered that prepared students with necessary skills for entry level jobs. Initial enrollment included 54 students who attended classes at different locations such as a house, Nuevo Liceo, the Black Star Line building, the

Vargas de Limón Park, the School for Girls, Alto de Correo de Limón, and other premises. By 1977, enrollment increased to 200 students. (University of Costa Rica website, n.d.)

Residents in Limón collaborated to address their common concerns of inadequate classroom accommodations for students at the Decentralized Limón Service. Through their committee's dedication and hard work, they convinced the Ministry of Public Works and Transportation to donate approximately 15 acres of land for a permanent site. In 1978, funding from the community, government, and UCR aided in the construction of a pavilion to house ten pre-fabricated classrooms. On April 21st, 1979, the University Council held a ceremony in Limón to decree the opening of the Regional Center of Limón, which was ratified a year later on April 19th, 1980. During the five-year construction phase, the institution's lack of suitable classroom space continued until the Rómulo Salas Headquarters was completed. Not only construction workers, but also students, faculty, and staff participated in building the headquarters. They devoted countless hours and were persistent in their efforts, even during weekends, to work hard towards completion of the building.

Over the years, several important changes have been made to the infrastructure of the campus which included paving the side streets and constructing a new library, multi-purpose classrooms, and student residences. Other changes throughout the years were the construction of a main access road to the campus. A bridge was built to connect student residences to campus premises for the convenience of walking back-and-forth. Additional classrooms and laboratories were constructed for the engineering division.

Now known as UCR Caribbean Headquarters, the university has an enrollment of approximately 1,500 students in one or more career programs. Programs include business management, public accounting, chemistry, customs administration, psychology, social work, business informatics, eco-tourism, pre-school education with concentration in English and English teaching. Master's degree programs are also offered.

UCR - Caribbean Headquarters in association with UCR's Development Observatory established the Observatory of Sustainable Tourism of the Caribbean (OBTUR-CARIBE) in May 2013. The main objective of OBTUR-CARIBE is to collect and generate information online on tourism throughout Limón Province and other coastal regions. Therefore, it serves as a research center for those who are interested in learning about how tourism relates to the coastal provinces, in particular Limón. The range of research topics include regulatory planning, land maritime zone planning, tourism, business environment, flora and fauna along with culinary arts. Data is gathered within the Limón Province from state institutions, non-governmental organizations, private companies, tourism organizations, trade and industry and other sources linked to tourism in Costa Rican's Caribbean region. UCR Caribbean Headquarters intends for OBTUR-CARIBE's research bank to be a valuable resource to their students enrolled in the ecotourism program. UCR Caribbean Headquarters has also developed partnerships with various international universities that support the initiatives of OBTUR-CARIBE.

The University of Costa Rica, in compliance with United Nations 64/460, began a 10-year research in 2013 to study and celebrate the international heritage of African people around the world. In so doing, the university has organized a series of yearly events throughout August in the Limón Province. The University of Costa Rica commemorates the annual celebrations of the Day of the Afro-Costa Rican culture with a series of activities such as workshops, exhibitions. Traditional events include the celebration of Marcus Garvey's birthday, a beauty pageant, a symposium on Afro-Costa Rican women and their political roles. Entertainment, parades, music, and family activities are popular aspects of the celebrations. Participation in the annual events are significant to those students and their professors who may spent an entire year planning cultural performances. But the events are not only concentrated in Limón and on the UCR Caribbean Campus. Traditional activities are also held in other towns in Limón Province, such as Siquirres, where there is a large Afro-Costa Rican population.

University College of Limón

In 1999, legal plans were approved to establish the University College of Limón (CUNLIMON) as a semi-autonomous higher education institution. CUNLIMON has been structured to offer short-term educational programs to prepare students for the labor market. Upon its opening in September 2002, class offerings have been aimed at those who are not seeking to enroll in the formal educational programs. So, the inaugural class included 44 students enrolled in the business computer course and 75 students in community based technical programs. Apart from these expected career and technical level diploma courses, students may also attend workshops that include self-improvement and professional development.

CUNLIMON, in agreement with the University of Costa Rica (UCR) Sede Limón, provides students with the opportunity to continue their education at UCR. Similarly, an agreement with the National Apprenticeship Institute (INA) provides CUNLIMON students with advanced training. Extensive expansion efforts have continued at CUNLIMON in opening headquarters in different communities throughout Limón Province to address career and technical educational needs.

CUNLIMON has also adapted their community education programs to the needs of production and business sectors in Limón Province. CUNLIMON form a partnership to develop workers' competency and employability skills by delivering programs revised for a specific business. Different methods of learning are conducted through presentations, workshops, conferences, and seminars. Workers may receive specialty training to learn employable skills that are required by the labor market to improve their job performance. Some may be expected by their leaders to bring back knowledge to the organization to train other workers to enhance the company's productivity. The technical programs consist of a maximum of 10 to 12 modules on topics such as language, technology and computer programs, organizational and business management, tourism, port management, fishing and aquaculture, improvement and physical development of the elderly.

Siquirres, Siquirres Municipality – Limón Province

Siquirres is the capital of the Siquirres Municipality in Limón Province. The rural, laid-back town has approximately 18,000 residents. Situated at the center of Limón Province at the foot of the Talamanca Mountain Range, the location of Siquirres signifies where the Atlantic great plain or Caribbean begins. The town was formed in conjunction with the development of the railway.

The population began to increase when workers migrated to Costa Rica to construct the Atlantic Railroad. More migrants moved to the town to also work on the banana farms during the 1930s and the cacao farms during the 1940s. Workers who immigrated to Siquirres came primarily from Jamaica. Many of their descendants continue to reside in the low-level town where farmers cultivate agricultural crops such as banana and pineapple. When the government enacted its apartheid practices against movements of Afro-Caribbean residents, Siquirres became the final western destination point where Limón Providence residents could travel. Any movements beyond Siquirres were against the restrictive laws of Costa Rica.

Siquirres is in one of the most accessible regions of Costa Rica. So, the town is used as a popular thoroughfare to get from the western capital city of San José to the eastern coast of Puerto de Limón, the most important port in Costa Rica. For the 3 to 4-hour drive, a great number of cargo trucks travels from San José through Siquirres en route to deliver supplies or pick up materials from Puerto de Limón, where more exports and imports go through than Puerto de Caldera in San José. Siquirres is also an important transportation hub for other towns located along the Highway 32 intersection with Highway 10. However, the status as a transportation hub was partially disrupted when trains travelling between Siquirres and Puerto de Limón were affected by the 1991 earthquake. This caused severe damages to the rails, and service has been discontinued since then. The lack of train service, however, has not deterred tourists from visiting Siquirres to enjoy rafting and kayaking on the town's Pacuare and Reventazon rivers.

Colegio Técnico Profesional
Padre Roberto Evans Saunders De Siquirres

In April 1963, the Siquirres Agricultural Institute was
officially opened. The institution was founded by Limón
born Father Robert Henry Evans Saunder who became the
school's first director. The capital town of Siquirres was
chosen as the school's location because of its centrally
located train stop. The first school was formerly housed in
a building owned by Standard Fruit Company on a property
located behind the railroad station. The school's
collaboration with a manager at Northern Railway
Company resulted in the company generously offering free
train rides to students. Even when the company could no
longer maintain the free travel, it still provided students
with discounted tickets.

The initial enrollment was 131 students who resided not
only in Siquirres but also in other communities outside of
Siquirres such as Pococí, Guácimo, and Matina. Upon
inception, the school teamed up with Costa Rica's first 4-H
Club, also known as 4-S Club, to teach courses in furniture
construction, sewing, agriculture, and clerical training.
During the mid-1970s, the school was relocated to the
Antonio Facio Elementary School premises, a larger
facility that would better accommodate the growing student
population. Also, on-campus housing was established for
236 students and later increased to accommodate the
housing of 64 additional students. In 1979, Father Evans
retired from the school's leadership post. He is remembered
for his contributions to the school and as the first Afro-
Costa Rican minister ordained by the Roman Catholic
Church of Costa Rica. Since 1986, the town of Siquirres
and the institution have celebrated Founder's Day every
November 7th in honor of Father Saunders and other
school founding members.

By 1982, enrollment totaled approximately 1300 students including those attending the newly opened night school for many young learners who, for various reasons, dropped out of the day school. On December 4th, 2000 the school became known as Padre Roberto Evans Saunders Professional Technical School. Currently, the secondary school has an enrollment of approximately 1750 students from grades 7 to 12. The teaching and administrative staff include 121 employees.

Further expansions resulted in the purchase of land that houses a physical plant, a pasture, forest reserve, and other infrastructure. This infrastructure is comprised of 60 classrooms, five administrative offices, a cellar, teachers' rooms, a gym, and dining room. Students use the fully equipped computer labs for computer science courses and English as a Second Language instruction. Other subjects taught inside classrooms include accounting and finance, eco-tourism, occupational health, fashion design, electrical technology.

The school also places an emphasis on agriculture and livestock. Goats, pigs, and dairy cattle are reared on the school's farm. In addition to agricultural cultivation on the spacious plot of land, students grow ornamental plants. The curriculum includes the agri-industry where students gain food processing experience to produce chips, cheese, and other items. Collaboration with external groups allows the institution to conduct Huerta workshops for guanabana and orange production and exploratory workshops for commercial chicken rearing.

References

ACLU (2010). *Lincoln University students and Chester County residents settle lawsuit charging racial discrimination in 2008 elections*. Retrieved from https://www.aclu.org/news/lincoln-university-students-and-chester-county-residents-settle-lawsuit-charging-racial on February 2nd, 2019

Akande, H. (2016). *Illuminating the Blackness: Blacks and African Muslims in Brazil*. Rabaah Publishers, London: England

Aldridge, D. & Young C. (2000). *Out of the Revolution: The Development of Africana Studies*. The Rowman & Littlefield Publishing Group, Inc. Lanham: MD

Archibold, R. (2013). *A nce-vibrant city struggles as Panama Ahead on a wave of prosperity*. Retrieved on April 15, 2019 from https://www.nytimes.com/2013/03/24/world/americas/frustrations-in-colon-panama-as-economic-growth-skirts-by.html

Arsenault and Rose, (2006). *Africa Enslaved: A Curriculum Unit on Comparative Slave Systems for Grades 9 -12*. Retrieved April 10, 2018 from https://liberalarts.utexas.edu/hemispheres/_files/pdf/ slavery/Slavery_in_Haiti.pdf

Associated Press (2015). *Cheyney University placed on probation over financial issues*. Retrieved on September 25, 2016 from http://www.pennlive.com/news/2015/12/cheyney_university probation.html

Aubel, M. (2011). *Affirmative Action in Higher Education and Afro-Descendant Women in Bahia, Brazil*. University of Kansas, Department of Latin American Studies

Bacchus, M. K. (2006). Education as and for legitimacy -
     Development in West Indian education between 1846 and
     1895. Wilfrid Laurier University Press. Waterloo: Canada

Bauza, V. (2002). Guantánamo is Caribbean melting pot. Orlando
     Sentinel. Retrieved February 8, 2019 from
     https://www.orlandosentinel.com/news/os-xpm-2002-02-
     04-0202040029-story.html

Bello & Aliaga (2017). *The slavery in the jurisdiction of Bayamo in
     the last two decades of the eighteenth century*. Caribbean of
     Social Sciences. ISSN: 2254-7630. Retrieved October,
     2018from
     http://www.eumed.net/rev/caribe/2017/12/esclavitu
     d-bayamo.html

Black Past (n.d.). *Kingston, Jamaica (1692 -)*. Retrieved June 29,
     2019 from
     https://www.blackpast.org/global- african-history/places-
     global-african-history/kingston-jamaica-1692/

Blouet, O (1980). To make society safe for freedom: Slave
     education in Barbados, 1823-33. Journal of Negro History,
     65, 2 (1980). Pp. 126-34

Bluefields Indian and Caribbean University website (n.d.). *History
of the university*. Retrieved December 7th, 2017 from
     http://www.bicu.edu.ni/en/proyecto-
     institucional/historia-de-la-universidad

Bonner, W., Freelain, S., et. al (2011) *The Sumner Story*, Morgan
     James Publishing, New York, NY.

Burch, A. (2007). The Miami Herald. Afro-Latin   Americans: A
     Rising Voice. Retrieved August, 2017 from
     http://media.miamiherald.com/multimedia/news/afr
     olatin/part1/index.html

Butchart, R. (2002). Freedmen's Education during Reconstruction. Retrieved on September 21,
    2016 from http://www.georgiaencyclopedia.org/articles/history-archaeology/freedmens-education-during-reconstruction

Campbell, C. (1997). Endless Education: Main Currents in the Education System of Modern Trinidad and Tobago 1939 – 1986. The Press University of the West Indies: Kingston, Jamaica

Campbell, C. (1996). *The Young Colonials: A Social History of Education in Trinidad and Tobago*. The Press University of the West Indies. Kingston: Jamaica

Carey, B. (2018). *Nashville needs to come to terms with its slave past*. Tennessean. Retrieved January 30, 2018 from https://www.tennessean.com/story/opinion/2018/07/20/nashville-needs-come-terms-its-slave-past/555111002/

Castillo Serrano, D (2002). Understanding Our Past in the School Experience. Retrieved May 20, 2018 from https://reliovistas.ucr.ac.cr/index.php/intersedes/article/view/860/921

Charier, (1999). *The festivals of San Benito in Venezuela: From saint of the slaves to cultural promoter*. Article abstract retrieved on November 11, 2018 from https://www.researchgate.net/publication/297857400_The_festivals_of_San_Benito_in_Venezuela_From_saint_of_the_slaves_to_cultural_promoter

Cheyney University. *The History of Cheyney University*. Retrieved September 20, 2016 from http://www.cheyney.edu/about-cheyney-university/cheyney-history.cfm

Chiodelli, F. (n.d.). *São Paulo, the Challenge of the Favelas.* Retrieved March, 2019 from http://www.planum.net/francesco-chiodelli-sao-paulo-the-challenge-of-the-favelas

Clio (n.d.). Sumner High School. Retrieved October 23, 2016 from https://www.theclio.com/web/entry?id=13412

Coleman, D. (n.d.). *The history of historically Black colleges and universities.* Retrieved September 22, 2016 from http://hbcuconnect.com/history.shtml

The Colonial Williamsburg Foundation (n.d.). *Dutch Slave Trade.* Retrieved September 11, 2018 from http://slaveryandremembrance.org/articles/article/?id=A0145

Committee on the Elimination of Racial Discrimination (2013). https://tbinternet.ohchr.org/Treaties/CERD/.../CERD_C_SUR_13-15_6576_E.doc

Common Fund (2009). *Case History: The Spelman College Endowment.* Retrieved February 24, 2018 from https://files.eric.ed.gov/fulltext/ED559306.pdf

Connell, J. (2017). *The political ecology of Maroon autonomy: land, resource extraction and political change in 21st century Jamaica and Suriname.* Retrieved September 9, 2018 from http://digitalassets.lib.berkeley.edu/etd/ucb/text/Connell_berkeley_0028E_17082.pdf

Consejo Superior Universitario Centroamericano (n.d.). *New university Member of CSUCA.* Bluefields Indian & Caribbean University -BICU-, Bluefields, Nicaragua, Retrieved December 4th, 2017 from http://www.csuca.org/index.php/219-bluefields-indian-caribbean-university-bicu-de-bluefields-nicaragua-nueva-universidad-miembro-del-csuca

Cottrol, R. (2013). *The Long, Lingering Shadow: Slavery, Race, and Law in the American Hemisphere*. University of Georgia Press. Athens:GA

Crouch, E. (2015). *Sumner celebrates its past amid worries about the future*. Retrieved October 23, 2016 from http://www.stltoday.com/news/local/education/sumner-celebrates-its-past-amid-worries-about-the-future/article_fa935619-5d64-5fb0-ab60-caecc76f0f92.html

The Daily Gleaner (1901). The first normal school in the Western Hemisphere. Retrieved February 4, 2017 from http://jamaica-history.weebly.com/the-mico.html

The Daily Gleaner (1911). The first government continuation school in Jamaica. Teaching of Technical and Commercial Subjects – Long felt need filled - Fitting Boys and Girls for Work of the Country. Retrieved July 13, 2018 from https://jamaica-history.weebly.com/kingston-technical-high-school.html

Darko Ankrah, K. (2013). Saramaka (Saramaccan) people: The fearless Suriname largest maroon tribe. Retrieved on September 13, 2018 from https://kwekudeeripdownmemorylane.blogspot.com/2013/06/saramaka-saramaccan-people-fearless.html

De la Fuente, A (2001). A nation for all (Envisioning Cuba). University of North Carolina Press. Chapel Hill: NC

Edgell, H. (2018). *St. Louis continues to lose black residents as white population makes a comeback*. Retrieved from http://news.stlpublicradio.org/post/st-louis-continues-lose-black-residents-white-population-makes-comeback#stream/0 on January 31st, 2019

Finkelman, P. (2009). *Encyclopedia of African American History, 1896 to the Present: From the Age of Segregation to the Twenty-first Century Five-volume set.* 1st edition. Oxford University Press: NY

Frazier, S. (2007). *Ethnicity, Empire, and Exclusion: The Incorporation of a Caribbean Borderland, 1893-1909.* http://lanic.utexas.edu/project/etext/llilas/ilassa/2007/frazier.pdf

Futhey & Cope (1881). *Slavery in Chester County.* Retrieved from https://www.chester.paroots.com/african_american_research/slavery.htm on February 2, 2019.

George, R. (n.d.). *What it means to be Black in Nashville, Tennessee.* Travel Noire. Retrieved January 30th, 2019 from https://travelnoire.com/what-its-like-to-be-black-in-nashville/

George Mason University (n.d.). *Histories of the National Mall.* Retrieved Jauuary 24th, 2019 from http://mallhistory.org/explorations/show/mall-slavery

Global Foundation to Upgrade Underserved Primary and Secondary School (n.d.). *Development of the education structure.* https://everychildcanachieve.org/caribbean-islands.html

Harrison A. (1982). *Piney Woods School an Oral History.* Jackson:University Press of Mississippi.

Instituto Brasil África (2017). *Salvador: The most African city in the world.* Atlantico. Retrieved March, 2019 from https://medium.com/atlantico-online/salvador-the-most-african-city-in-the-world-b93673215231

Ishmael, O (2014). The Guyana story: From earliest times to independence. Retrieved July 27, 2015 from http://www.guyana.org/features/guyanastory/chapter59.html

Hansen, A. (1962. *George W. Hubbard Hospital, 1910-1961.*
        Journal of the National Medical Association. January, 1962
        Vol. 54 No. 1

Hawkins, D. (2017). *In Cuba, African Roots Run Deep, but It's a
        Lesson Students Aren't Learning in the Classroom.*
        Retrieved October 13, 2017 from
        https://www.nbcnews.com/news/nbcblk/cuba-african-roots-
        run-deep-it-s-lesson-students-aren-n767616

Herrera, S. (2012). *A history of violence and exclusion: Afro-
        Colombian from slavery to displacement.* Retrieved
        December 21, 2018 from
        https://repository.library.georgetown.edu/bitstream/handle/
        10822/557698/Herrera_georgetown_0076M_11964.pdf;seq
        uence=1

Jacobs, P. (2015). *There's an unprecedented crisis facing America's
        historically Black colleges.* Retrieved September 22, 2016
        from http://www.businessinsider.com/hbcus-may-be-more-
        in-danger-of-closing-than-other-schools-2015-3

Kambel, E. and MacKay (1999). The rights of indigenous peoples
        and Maroons in Suriname. International Work Group for
        Indigenous Affairs Publishing. Copenhagen: Denmark

Kashatus, W. (2002). *Just over the line: Chester County and the
        underground railroad.* Chester County Historical Society

King, R. (1998). Education in the British Caribbean: The legacy of
        the nineteenth century. Retrieved on July 27, 2016 from
        https://www.educoas.org/Portal/bdigital/contenido/interame
        r/BkIACD/Interamer/Interamerhtml/Millerhtml/mil_king.ht
        m

Klein, H. (1978). The english slave trade to Jamaica, 1782-1808.
        The Economic History Review,
        Vol. 31, Issue 1, 25-45.

Koops, B.J., Oosterlaken, et. al. (2015). *Responsible Innovation 2: Concepts, Approaches, and Applications*. Responsible Innovation 2. Springer International Publishing, Switzerland

Kotkin, J. and Cox, W. (2018). *The cities where African Americans are doing the best economically 2018*. Forbes online. Retrieved on January 30, 2019 from https://www.forbes.com/sites/joelkotkin/2018/01/15/the-cities-where-african-americans-are-doing-the-best-economically-2018/#1d6c19a71abe

Layne, A. (2002). St. Leonard's Boys Secondary School's 50th Anniversary Lecture. Retrieved June, 2017 from http://www.butbarbados.com/wp-content/uploads/sites/22/2018/05/speech5.pdf

Leiner, M, Cuba's schools: 25 years later, in Halebsky, S. and Kirk, J.M. (eds.) Cuba: Twenty-five Years of Revolution, 1959-1984, New York, Praeger 1985.

The Lodge School Early History (nd). Retrieved August 29, 2016 from http://www.liquisearch.com/the_lodge_school/early_history_1745_to_1880

Lovett, B. (1999). The African-American History of Nashville, Tennessee, 1780-1930: Elites and Dilemmas (Black Community Studies). University of Arkansas Press. Fayetteville:AR

Mangar, T. (2009). *The evolution of an education system in 19th century Colonial British Guiana: From the Dutch to British compulsory education ordinance of 1876*. Stabraek News, Guyana

Martinez, J. and Diaz, C. (2014) *Veroes Municipality - Development of Culture*. Retrieved October 12, 2018 from http://josemighell.blogspot.com/2014/06/desarrollo-de-la-cultura-fundamento.html

Meditz, W. and Hanratty, D. (1987). *Caribbean Islands: A Country Study. Washington: GPO for the Library of Congress.*

McAlmont, C. The African Village Movement. Retrieved August 1st, 2018 from https://www.stabroeknews.com/2013/news/guyana/08/01/the-african-village-movement-2/

McLucas, K. L (2005) *Race and Inequality in Brazil: The Afro-Brazilian Struggle in the Racial Democracy.* Retrieved October 18, 2017 from file:///C:/Users/254567/Downloads/88-227-1-PB.pdf

McQuirter, M. (2003). *A brief history of African Americans in Washington, D.C. African American heritage trail. African Americans in Washington, DC: 1800-1975.* Retrieved from https://www.culturaltourismdc.org/portal/a-brief-history-of-african-americans-in-washington-dc

Migge, B. Leglise, I., Barten, A (2010). *Creoles in Education: An appraisal of current and projects (Creole Language Library).* John Benjamins Publishing Company. Amsterdam: Netherlands

Miller, E. (1990). Jamaican society and high schooling. Mona, Jamaica: Institute of Social and Economic Research.

National Park Service (2015). *African-American life in St. Louis, 1804-1865.* Retrieved from https://www.nps.gov/jeff/learn/historyculture/african-american-life-in-saint-louis-1804-through-1865.htm on January 31st, 2019

The New Georgia Encyclopedia (2006). Morehouse College. https://www.georgiaencyclopedia.org/articles/education/morehouse-college. Retrieved July 4, 2018

Tyrrell-Kellman, N. (n.d.). *Pioneers of education.* Retrieved on July 14, 2018 from http://www.buxtonguyana.net/index_files/Page398.htm

Nittle, N. (2017. Atlanta Black Star. How Afro-Nicaraguans Suffer Through the 'Taboo' Subject of Racism. Retrieved August, 2017 from http://atlantablackstar.com/2017/07/30/afro-nicaraguans-suffer-taboo-subject-racism/

Ogilvie, D. (n.d.). *The history of the parish of Trelawny*. Retrieved on July 13, 2018 from http://www.jamaicanfamilysearch.com/Samples/histre06.htm

Pamphile, L. (2008). *Clash of Cultures: America's Educational Strategies in Occupied Haiti, 1915-1934*. University Press of America, Inc., New York: NY

Pitsch, M. and Ritzenthaler, R. (2001). Autonomy Tale. Report from Bluefields, Nicaragua. Resource Center of the Americas. Retrieved November 3, 2017 from http://insidecostarica.com/specialreports/nicaragua_automony_tale.htm

Puerto Viejo Satellite, (n.d.). *Learning, Schools and the Education System in the South Caribbean of Costa Rica*. Retrieved from https://www.puertoviejosatellite.com/education.php on January 12, 2019

Randeraad, N (1998). *Mediators between state and society*. Verloren Publishers: Rotterdam, Netherlands

Rivers, L. (1981). *Slavery in Microcosm: Leon County, Florida, 1824 to 1860*, The Journal of Negro History, Vol. 66, No. 3 (Autumn, 1981), pp. 235-245,.

Rodríguez, Alfonso & Cavelier. (2009*). Race and human rights in Colombia. Inform about racial discrimination and rights of the Afro-Colombian population* Lombard Nomos Impresores, Bogotá, 2009.

Rosales, F. (2003). *Rescuing the "children of the drug"*. La Prensa. Retrieved on November 4, 2017 from https://www.laprensa.com.ni/2003/05/07/nacionales/86243 2-rescatando-a-los-hijos-de-la-droga

Ruelas, A. (2017). *How African Americans emerged from slavery with a hunger for education.* Retrieved on June 29th, 2018 from http://www.zocalopublicsquare.org/2017/07/28/african-americans-emerged-slavery-hung

Sanchez, G. (1963). The Development of Education in Venezuela. Office of Education (DHEW) Washington, D.C., Bull-1963-7; OF-14086

Sangster, A. (2011). The making of a university: from CAST to Utech. Ian Randle Publishers, Jamaica

Sierra, J. (n.d.). *End of slavery in Cuba*. Retrieved from http://www.historyofcuba.com/history/race/EndSlave.htm on June 4, 2018

Simkin, J. (2015). Education of Slaves. Retrieved on April 29, 1018 from http://spartacus-educational.com/USASeducation.htm

SocialistWorker (n.d.). Sugar and slavery exhibition: were there really any kindly slave owners? Retrieved January 22, 2019 from https://socialistworker.co.uk/art/11161/Sugar+and+Slavery +exhibition%3A+were+there+really+any+kindly+slave+o wners

Spartacus Educational (n.d.). Education of slaves. Retrieved July 26, 2016 from http://spartacus-educational.com/USASeducation.htm

Spinell, L. (2013). New Dunbar High School on track for next fall. Retrieved October 15, 2016 from http://www.elevationdcmedia.com/devnews/dunbarhighsch ool_052113.aspx

StateUniversity.com (n.d.) Hiiti History & Background. Retrieved
July 11, 2017from
http://education.stateuniversity.com/pages/596/Haiti-
HISTORY-BACKGROUND.html

StateUniversity.com (n.d.) Suriname - Summary. Retrieved
Decembber 15, 2017 from
http://education.stateuniversity.com/pages/1447/Suriname-
SUMMARY.html

Steljn, J. (2013). *Dutch slavery: Our darkest past.* Retrieved April
13, 2019 from
https://dutchreview.com/featured/dutch-slavery-our-dark-
past/

The History of Secondary Education and the Development of
Curricula (n.d.). *Chapter IV. The
secondary school system of Trinidad and Tobago.*
Retrieved July 13, 2018 from
http://www.educoas.org/Portal/bdigital/contenido/interamer
/BkIACD/Interamer/Interamerhtml/Alleynehtml/AllCh4.ht
m

Thomas, E. (2014). *Education in the commonwealth Caribbean and
Netherlands Antilles.* Bloombury Publishing. London: UK

Tinker Salas, M. The Enduring Legacy (2009). *The enduring
legacy: Oil, Culture, and Society in Venezuela.* Durnham:
NC. Duke University Press.

Tyson, C. (2014). *For Storied Institution, a Historic Low.* Retrieved
September 25, 2016 from
https://www.insidehighered.com/news/2014/06/30/wilberfo
rce-university-countrys-oldest-private-historically-black-
institution-could

University of the Autonomous Regions of the Nicaraguan
Caribbean Coast (n.d.) *Institutional Historical Review.*
Retrieved on December 4, 2017 from
http://www.uraccan.edu.ni/content/rese%C3%B1a-
hist%C3%B3rica-institucional

University of the Autonomous Regions of the Nicaraguan
    Caribbean Coast (n.d.) *Review Bluefields Precinct.*
    Retrieved on December 5th, 2017 from
    http://www.uraccan.edu.ni/content/rese%C3%B1a-recinto-
    bluefields

University of Costa Rica (n.d.). Historical Review. Retrieved April,
    2018 from
    http://sedecaribe.ucr.ac.cr/index.php/resena-historica-ver-
    mas

U.S. Department of Education (1991). *Historically Black Colleges
    and Universities and Higher Education Desegregation.*
    Retrieved September 22, 2016 from
    http://www2.ed.gov/about/offices/list/ocr/docs/hq9511.htm
    l

Virlarys (2015). Community of Farriar Veroes. Retrieved on
    October 12, 2018 from
    https://translate.google.com/translate?hl=en&sl=es&u=http
    s://www.clubensayos.com/Biograf%25C3%25ADas/COM
    UNIDAD-DE-FARRIAR-
    VEROES/2293855.html&prev=search

Williams, H. (2005). Self-taught: African American education in
    slavery and freedom. Chapel Hill: University of North
    Carolina Press p. 320.

Woodhouse, K. (2015). An HBCU fights to survive. Inside Higher
    Ed. Retrieved September 23,
    2016 from
    https://www.insidehighered.com/news/2015/09/15/problem
    s-mount-cheyney-university-oldest-hbcu
    https://books.google.com/books?id=rTfRCwAAQBAJ&pg
    =PA104&lpg=PA104&dq=favela+secondary+schools,&so
    urce=bl&ots=ncYce11Xza&sig=QOAHfxvLDlRBuvu6Lig
    cV8LLTb4&hl=en&sa=X&ved=0ahUKEwiv6pvto6DXAh
    UETCYKHeZfDNkQ6AEIUjAI#v=onepage&q=favela%2
    0secondary%20schools%2C&f=false

Segregation has no place in the
education system.

~Richard Dawkins

www.ingramcontent.com/pod-product-compliance
Lightning Source LLC
Chambersburg PA
CBHW051434250726
48655CB00001B/60